MW00808200

PRAISE FOR *PUTTING IT ALL TOGETHER: CREATING AND SCALING EXCEPTIONAL LEARNING*

We are certain that learners and teachers benefit from communities of practice but sometimes we fail to act on that certainty and we leave individuals to heavy lift of organizational change. However, within this understanding, *Putting It All Together*'s approach offers us research-informed strategies for systemic, substantive change within the context of learning communities. It is in these communities of practice that risks are invited, change supported, and collaboration enabled. It is also within these communities that I find great hope in what might be possible as we consider making a difference, not one person at a time but rather, one team at a time.

Although considerable literature exists on the need for change in educational environments, many of those calls for change either forget or dismiss the power that can be generated from communities of practice as a lever for change. Teaching and leading can be lonely enterprises. This work acknowledges that sustained and meaningful change is possible when conversations are invited and communities are present, resulting in transformed cultures. The result is not just one change or another, but a culture shift. That possibility is exciting.

—Zach Kelehear, Ed.D., professor and Vice Provost, Augusta University

Effective teaching and student learning are living art and science. This concept is demonstrated in *Putting It All Together: Creating and Scaling Exceptional Learning.* The collection is an excellent resource for ideas on how to improve student learning and scale efforts to positively impact as many students as possible, whether within a single institution or a system of colleges and universities. The thematically arranged case studies allow the reader to understand that while there is no "one size fits all," there are myriad approaches that can be taken to create exceptional learning environments. The content also highlights that collaboration can create synergies between faculty, staff, and administration within institutions, across institutions, and even across an entire university system.

**—Rob Page, Vice President for Academic and Student Affairs,
South Georgia State College**

Through its insightful examination of faculty learning communities, *Putting It All Together: Creating and Scaling Exceptional Learning* sheds light on the transformative power of innovative pedagogical practices in enhancing student success. Its compelling narrative and practical guidance inspire educators to engage in collaborative learning, leading to a deepened commitment to student-centered teaching and learning. A must-read for all those who are passionate about empowering students and creating a more inclusive and equitable learning environment.

—Jessica Traylor, Ph.D., assistant professor of psychology, Gordon State College

Virtually everyone who works in higher education is theoretically dedicated to deepening student learning, but the reality of bringing such a lofty goal to fruition on a large scale can be daunting. *Putting It All Together: Creating and Scaling Exceptional Learning* is perfectly titled because it does just that; it provides what is required to move individuals and institutions from idea to implementation by providing what is most needed to make that leap: concrete examples *and* attention to the whole spectrum of courses, programs, and entire general education curricula. I highly recommend this opportunity to learn from those who are already doing it.

—Cynthia J. Alby, Ph.D.; professor of teacher education, Georgia College; and author of *Learning That Matters: A Field Guide to Course Design for Transformative Education*

Putting It All Together

Putting It All Together

Creating and Scaling Exceptional Learning

Jeffery W. Galle and Jo K. Galle

ROWMAN & LITTLEFIELD
Lanham • Boulder • New York • London

Published by Rowman & Littlefield
An imprint of The Rowman & Littlefield Publishing Group, Inc.
4501 Forbes Boulevard, Suite 200, Lanham, Maryland 20706
www.rowman.com

86-90 Paul Street, London EC2A 4NE, United Kingdom

British Library Cataloguing in Publication Information Available

Library of Congress Cataloging-in-Publication Data

Names: Galle, Jeffery, author. | Galle, Jo K., 1957– author.
Title: Putting it all together : creating and scaling exceptional learning / Jeffery W. Galle and Jo K. Galle.
Description: Lanham : Rowman and Littlefield, [2023] | Includes bibliographical references. | Summary: "The purpose is to provide the evidence-based practices and the faculty learning community program as the vehicle for massive innovation across three contexts-courses, programs, and the General Education Program and undergraduate curriculum"—Provided by publisher.
Identifiers: LCCN 2023011826 | ISBN 9781475867954 (cloth) | ISBN 9781475867961 (paperback) | ISBN 9781475867978 (epub)
Subjects: LCSH: College teaching—Georgia. | Professional learning communities—Georgia. | General education—Georgia. | Universities and colleges—Curricula—Georgia. | Education, Higher—Aims and objectives—Georgia. | University System of Georgia.
Classification: LCC LB2331 .G355 2023 | DDC 378.1/250973—dc23/eng/20230420
LC record available at https://lccn.loc.gov/2023011826

Contents

Foreword

Working with colleagues across the University System of Georgia (USG) as Chief Academic Officer (CAO) and Executive Vice Chancellor, prior to my current position in Louisiana, was an enlightening and rewarding experience. A focused commitment to student success began more than a decade ago with the initial Complete College Georgia projects. When I arrived in 2017, the institutions were primed for a significant collective movement forward with the implementation of the first comprehensive system-scale student success strategy, the Momentum Year. As they implemented this framework of evidence based strategies on their campuses, I saw first-hand the creative responses by the institutional leadership in revising the way that developmental education was done, in introducing new practices of lowering costs for students, in revising advising, and most key perhaps, in greatly modifying the way the first year of college was being structured for students.

Yet, structural institutional change, while important, is only the beginning. Change must happen at the institutional, curricular, program, and of course classroom level. Consequently, Academic Affairs at the System Office also explored ways to work with USG faculty to introduce pedagogical innovation at the course level through the Chancellor's Learning Scholars (CLS) program. With the support of each Teaching and Learning center within each institution and the Academic Affairs team at the Board, we fashioned a faculty learning program that created more than 250 communities of practice, involving almost 3,000 faculty, across every public college and university. The work of this group resulted in innovative pedagogy being directly embedded in more than 25,000 courses.

Putting It All Together: Creating and Scaling Exceptional Learning Experiences captures the experience of a large number of the USG's leading faculty, many of whom served as facilitators of individual learning communities in the CLS program. Now a year or more later, these faculty and many administrators can update their course impact and program changes in individual brief snapshot narratives.

The conviction of the author/editor Jeffery Galle was that select strategies and activities frame the content of courses and programs so as to welcome and engage all students to join the academic community. This book underscores the conviction that *how* we engage students is foundational to their learning the disciplinary content of the courses and programs. That is to say, the more than thirty authors in this volume have discovered that student engagement is fundamental to learning in multiple contexts. Students and our institutions succeed because of the way we interact with each other. The data at every level clearly support the impact of this approach.

This volume of thirty-four essays encourages educators to meet the challenge of maintaining both rigor and welcome, to engage each student where deep learning can take place. The institutions represented by faculty and administrator authors not only range across the USG but have significant representation from research institutions such as Emory and Rice as well as out of state institutions such as Lenoir-Rhyne. It is truly remarkable that the individual narratives across such a range of faculty and administrators are all giving momentum to student engagement through developing innovative courses and engaging programs.

The collection has been designed to gather together as many voices as possible, so these essays are snapshots of individual and collective efforts, which taken together make a single point: every professional, every office, every individual within an institution can contribute to the successful learning of students.

Tristan Denley, Ph.D.
Deputy Commissioner for
Academic Affairs and Innovation
Louisiana Board of Regents

Preface

Jeffery Galle

For faculty, the love of one's discipline and area of expertise naturally leads to sharing the discipline with students. The sharing takes on the colors and hues of learning when a student's response indicates, "I've got it!"

As we as faculty and administrators have learned, to make the ideal happen over and over, so much new learning and relearning must occur. And by the faculty themselves, not only students. All too often, the challenges seem to overmatch the successes.

Teaching and teachers face numerous serious challenges today from the pandemic and its effects as well as the interference of political rhetoric spilling over into the classroom and the curriculum.

The disconnect between the original passion of faculty for their discipline and the facts of inadequate student learning, their progression, and graduation shows the gap between where faculty thrive and where they often find themselves. Add to these conditions the serious critiques of serious educators such as Derek Bok whose *Our Underachieving Colleges* directs a critical eye on the outcomes of undergraduate education.

This is why a book that foregrounds the "teaching moves" that faculty can make is necessary.[1]

Add to that idea the possibility that such pedagogies (a fancier word for "teaching moves") may actually be quite useful and good in other contexts beyond the classroom, and one can sense the unarticulated power of good teaching.

Indeed, Derek Bok himself, often cited for tracing the current and historical missteps of higher education in great detail, actually argues that the "most of the serious deficiencies can be overcome, at least to a significant degree, given the will to do so."[2]

Much of the pedagogical and learning science work of the past twenty years clearly indicates the will to remedy underachievement is present. The good news is higher education has the resources and tools to address the challenges of the pandemic, politics, and underachievement. We know much more about the ways students learn experientially and collaboratively. We have developed practices and pedagogies that enliven and engage students and invite learning. The contexts within which faculty work are involved—from course design to the classroom, to the lab, and out to the world where experiential learning can occur most richly.

The unfortunate news is the resources and tools are not often organized in such a way as to make them accessible to all faculty. Also, the patchwork nature of the teaching and learning landscape invites a publication that has done the work of selecting specific tools and resources supported by learning science, and of soliciting narratives from many experts, narratives across courses, programs, and curricula that successfully place these pedagogies and practices in action. Faculty and administrators also need learning materials that are cutting edge, evidence-based, and applicable to multiple contexts within which faculty and administrators find themselves at work.

In short, what can be most useful to meet the urgent needs of the present challenges is an organized framework of theory and praxis—essentially a short list of the most impactful evidence-based practices and pedagogies accompanied by a compendium of brief applications of the practices and pedagogies.

Courses, programs, and the curriculum are three of the most essential academic areas in which important work for students is undertaken. Embedding the most powerful practices and pedagogies within courses, programs, and the curriculum calls for every professional at every institution to play a different but equally important role in improving student learning and student success. Thus, if remedies for the challenges of the pandemic, politics, and historical underachievement can be employed at every level—the course, the program, the curriculum, and even the state system—then higher education will be creating a vast pedagogical network composed of all professionals dedicated to deepening student learning and student success.

NOTES

1. The term "teaching moves" traces to my reading of the term writing "moves" that professional writers make. As creative professionals, it is reasonable to modify the term to fit teaching. From the excellent book *They Say / I Say* by Gerald Graff and Cathy Birkenstein.

2. Derek Bok, *Our Underachieving Colleges: A Candid Look at How Much Students Learn and Why They Should be Learning More* (Princeton: Princeton University Press, 2006), 10.

Introduction

Jeffery Galle

Much has been done to deepen the learning of undergraduate students and to enhance the prospect of their earning a degree, but the strategies and activities, essentially the content of the reform, have not been made easily available to the majority of professionals in such a way as to result in institutional level redesign of courses, programs, and the curriculum. Now, we have both the content of innovation and a mechanism for change in a campus wide program of well-supported faculty learning communities that are led by selected facilitators who have been recognized as excellent teachers.

The purpose of *Putting It All Together: Creating and Scaling Exceptional Learning*[1] is to provide the evidence-based practices and the faculty learning community program as the vehicle for massive innovation across three contexts—courses, programs (including student life and academic life), and the General Education Program and undergraduate curriculum. Each of the book's three segments begins with a framing chapter by the editors which is followed by the brief individual narratives by contributing authors.

By limiting length of submissions and creating specific topics for contributors to address, *Putting It All Together* presents the voices of many experts— faculty, staff, and administrators—all organized around the theme of innovating changes to deepen student learning and success. The primary drivers of change are the advances in how learning happens, particularly mindset strategies, inclusive pedagogy, classroom activities, student assignments, the High-Impact Practices, and assessment of learning. These advances can lead not only to learning through enriched courses, but also to learning within an array of other programs including the General Education Program and the undergraduate curriculum.

Course innovation has been the subject of many recent books, including Ken Bain's *Super Courses: The Future of Teaching and Learning*. What is additionally compelling about *Putting It All Together* is the extension of key practices and activities that faculty are already using in their courses to many programs and to the General Education Program and programs of study. The importance of these activities and strategies to learning warrants their being embedded in every facet of the academic community, and indeed with this book, there is a path forward to making that happen.

One method which can be used to gather data for a study such as this is to gather and analyze responses to a survey. Instead, individual contributions from administrators and faculty were sought, and the best of the subsequent submissions that were received contained individual voices that were so compelling that these unique faculty and administrators' contributions had such significant impact that each of these voices has been retained in this study.

Hence, the shape of the book is now an individual framing chapter before three individual contexts which successively are courses, programs, and the curriculum. In this way, individual narratives provide data and the immediate impact of their changes and innovation. The institutions represented range from small state colleges to major research institutions with comprehensive and state universities represented as well.

Accordingly, chapter 1 provides an overview of the most impactful pedagogical practices and activities mentioned above. These include course design, academic inquiry, mindset strategies, inclusive pedagogy, classroom engagement activities, the High-Impact Practices, transparent student assignments (the Purpose, Tasks, and Criteria of TiLT), and the assessment of learning techniques. Essentially, the first chapter sets out the menu of content to be used throughout the book and frames the essays of the first segment, course level innovation. Beginning with L. Dee Fink's Integrated Course Design, editors flesh out Fink's five elements by applying recent advances in learning science. The pedagogies of engagement listed above each receives some description or definition as well.

Chapters 2–20 offer individual contributions involving course innovation. These brief narratives are the selected responses to the invitation extended to faculty in a network of participants in programs ranging from the University System of Georgia's Chancellor's Learning Scholars program to Oxford College of Emory's Institute for Pedagogy in the Liberal Arts to the University System of Georgia's Chancellor's Learning Scholars (CLS) program.

Successive chapters are organized by central pedagogies in the order listed originally in this introduction. Hence, course design itself becomes the central topic of chapter 2 by Jim Fatzinger of Elon University. In chapter 3, Rebecca Harrison of University of West Georgia, describes academic inquiry and the identification of mistakes being used to develop new mental models.

Then a group of chapters employs a number of mindset and inclusive strategies and activities. Julie Kozee of Georgia Highland College focuses on facilitating belonging in first year composition (chapter 4). Veena Paliwal, University of West Georgia, in chapter 5 employs the idea of learning from mistakes in the calculus classes she teaches. In chapter 6 three faculty of the University of North Georgia (Lindsay Bailey, Shane Toepfer, and Laura Ng) employ a specific community-building technique to foster belonging. Molly Zhou of Dalton State College, in chapter 7, describes her use of the circle as an inclusive and belonging exercise.

In chapter 8, a good transition to classroom engagement strategies, Carl J. Gabrini, University of West Georgia, describes how learning every student's name in a large class sparks participation and confidence on their part. In chapter 9, Marlene Call of Brenau University, unveils a number of classroom activities that function to dispel anxiety, engage curiosity, and foster community in class. Clarence Riley at Fort Valley State University details in chapter 10 how first day activities invite students to engage with each other, the course content, and to shape the course from the first day.

Tracing back to course design, Sutandra Sarkar, of Georgia State University, in chapter 11, employs a number of small changes to heighten the impact of her math courses. In another disciplinary-based essay, Aubrey L. Dyer at Clayton State University describes in chapter 12 the use of peer learning assistants in the chemistry classroom. In a cogent essay in chapter 13, Emily G. Weigel of Georgia Tech describes engaging students in evidence-based practices in her course that involves analyzing evidence. In chapter 14, also anchored in the discipline, Monica Carol Miller describes how using professional interviews with attorneys conveys to students the breadth of the legal profession.

Three successive chapters focus on the use of a High-Impact Practice to engage students. Stefanie Sevcik of Georgia College and State University, in chapter 15, employs service learning for social justice in her general education courses. Sutandra Sarkar of Georgia State University, in chapter 16, describes the way a virtual exchange enhances collaboration and learning in her precalculus course. In chapter 17, Belinda P. Edwards advocates for writing as a way to foster deeper learning in mathematics.

Three more chapters to round out the faculty course contributions include chapter 18 and Ava Hogan-Chapman's use of Google Docs to nurture self-reflection and self-explanation for her Georgia Gwinnett College students. In chapter 19, Laura McCloskey Wolfe of the University of West Georgia fosters creativity and critical thinking through inquiry in the arts classroom. In chapter 20, Robert R. Bleil of the College of Coastal Georgia describes how his faculty learning community developed strategies to lessen

xx   *Introduction*

the degree of friction between students and faculty by adjusting out of class readings.

The second segment of the book begins with chapter 21 which frames the possibility of integrating one or more of the eight sets of strategies into an institution's programs. The chapter begins with a number of institutional and national programs that already possess a degree of success. The analysis suggests that these and other programs are conducive to further enrichment by the practices and activities that revolutionize the learning within courses.

Chapters 22 through chapter 31 are authored by administrators and faculty serving different institutions ranging from Emory University, Rice University, Georgia State University, to a number of state universities and colleges in Georgia and North Carolina.

In chapter 22, Jesse Bishop of Georgia Highland College lays the foundation for program improvement through an effective data communication. Two succeeding chapters focus on the development of inclusion in a thriving DEI program at two very different institutions. First, in chapter 23, Devon Fisher and Jessica O'Brien describe a program at Lenoir-Rhyne University that utilizes the power of listening. Second, in chapter 24, Donna Troka of Emory University's Center for Faculty Development and Excellence details a number of efforts of Emory's teaching center to foreground inclusion, diversity, and equity.

In chapter 25, Tyler Yu, Dean of Business at Georgia Gwinnett College, focuses on the development of individual High-Impact Practices across four centers he founded at his college. Then, in chapters 26 and 27, two more institutional leaders offer chapters on the development of a particular High-Impact Practice program. Frank Mendelson charts the reinvigoration of Savannah State University's First Year Experience program in chapter 26. At South Georgia State College, the Undergraduate Research Symposium's growth is detailed by Robert L. Potter, Rosa Guedes, and Frank Holiwski, in chapter 27.

New Faculty Orientation, New Faculty Academy, and Graduate Student Fellows Program provide three more examples of excellent opportunities to integrate innovative pedagogy as new faculty and graduate assistants are welcomed to an institution. Accordingly, Laura R. Lynch of the College of Coastal Georgia, in chapter 28, describes the focus on mindset of her New Faculty Orientation program. Then, in chapter 29, Ania Kowalik, assistant director of the teaching center at Rice University, describes in depth the best teaching practices that graduate teaching assistants share in her new graduate teaching program. In chapter 30, Mei Zhang describes a year-long academy offered to new faculty by her teaching center at Georgia Gwinnett College.

Chapter 31 presents an opportunity for cross-disciplinary collaboration in regard to teaching excellence. Laura Kim Gosa of Albany State University presents this model as a pilot project.

Two chapters form the third segment of *Putting It All Together*. Chapter 32 provides the frame for integrating innovative pedagogies within the General Education Program, new degree programs, and the undergraduate curriculum, as I also offer the work of Oxford College of Emory University to create its Ways of Inquiry GEP for Emory students in the first two years of study. Then, Associate Provost Jordan Cofer describes GC Journeys, the High-Impact Practices curriculum of Georgia College and State University, in chapter 33.

In the book's final chapter, I underscore the advantages to student learning offered by further integration of pedagogical innovation in courses, programs, and the curriculum.

NOTE

1. A note on the use of the term "scale" should be made early. The term is widely used in student success programs to signify the process of applying a good idea within an institution to all of the institutions in a state or in a national program. With the development of the networks prevalent today, the question of how new ideas can travel across an entire network has also become an important question. By using faculty and professional development within each institution, the network being forged across the University System of Georgia, and the national Professional and Organization Development network (POD), individuals can easily connect to resources and such programs as the learning communities program. What we are finding now is the meaning of "scale" is to join multiple networks in meaningful ways.

PART I

Pedagogies of Engagement within Courses

Chapter 1

Pedagogies of Engagement

"Teaching Moves" for Student Learning

Jeffery Galle

At the University System of Georgia (USG) from 2018 through 2021, there was an emergence of a data stream originating from within hundreds of faculty learning communities, each exploring a central pedagogy of engagement. Many of the resulting course changes made by faculty in the USG and described in detail in their year-end reports confirmed the importance of the "teaching moves" that faculty can make.[1]

Just as Gerald Graff and Cathy Birkenstein maintain that professional writers can make various "writing moves" that will improve the quality of their compositions, there are important "teaching moves" that faculty can implement which will result in deepening student learning. In addition to the course changes of participating faculty, two books also emerged from the USG's system wide program.[2] The program ended too soon, but lasted long enough to demonstrate the potential for good changes when small groups of faculty led by supported facilitators meet regularly on pedagogical topics of great importance to improving teaching.

In some ways, this new book connects to the work of the previous learning community project. Many of the authors, though not all, participated in the Chancellor's Learning Scholars program. The unit of measure remains the individual course, at least in this first section of the book, and most of the central pedagogical approaches have been retained. Faculty within the Georgia system of institutions are fortunate to have a consortium of teaching and learning leaders, the centers of teaching and learning directors, who form a powerful network of expertise and creative servant leadership.

PEDAGOGIES OF ENGAGEMENT

The names of the pedagogies may be familiar—integrated course design, academic inquiry, mindset strategies, inclusive strategies, class engagement activities, the High-Impact Practices, learner-centered assignments, and assessment of learning. The associated practices and strategies of these pedagogical areas can be thought of as Pedagogies of Engagement. What if all faculty teaching all courses possessed these eight elements in a rich mixture appropriate for each course? This is not impossible to imagine.

Course design/redesign viewed as the creation of significant learning experiences figures prominently in the work of L. Dee Fink.[3] His comprehensive approach to the integration of course components—situational factors, learning goals, learning activities, feedback and student assessments—established the gold standard for course design. Employing this process is beneficial both for new courses and the improvement of existing ones.

Originally called Backward Design because Fink began with the learning outcomes and worked "backward" to the assignments and the arrangement of content, the approach developed further, integrating five kinds of elements that led to the more apt term, Integrated Course Design. Fink's contribution has been invaluable to faculty teaching in face to face, online, and hybrid modalities as the course templates used to design courses in these modalities have been influenced by the Integrated Design approach.

One key process that university courses possess, no matter the discipline or course design, is academic inquiry. Similar to the scientific method, academic inquiry is followed by all academic areas to produce knowledge. The process of inquiry involves hypothesis testing by data gathering, analysis of results, and ultimately the confirmation or refutation of the hypothesis, and establishing knowledge as currently understood. In teaching and learning, faculty come up against the previous mental models that students bring to class. The work of inquiry then includes the identification of faulty mental models and the support of students in creating new paradigms. This is one of the situational factors that L. Dee Fink may not have anticipated but is nevertheless important to excellent teaching and course design.

More recent work can also enrich the course design effort. Several key categories of Fink—learning activities, feedback and assessment, and situational factors—all carry new and richer meanings now thanks to advances in learning science. Much more is available today that early proponents of Fink's work simply did not possess.

Carol Dweck's foundational work with Mindset, the current work of Mary Murphy, and a number of learning science experiments such as those conducted by Motivate Lab, represent significant landmarks in the growing focus on student motivation and learning. These advances can change how we construct learning experiences, how we teach, and, indeed, how units across an institution may include human motivation and human interactions in their programs and extended work.

Fundamental mindset concepts include the idea that evidence supports that intelligence is not fixed; rather, it changes with motivation, and it can grow with effective discovery and analysis of mistakes. How faculty design activities, what faculty say, essentially how faculty communicate with students can influence how they learn. Additionally, making mistakes is now viewed as integral to the learning process; learning with a growth, as opposed to a fixed, mindset may affect chances for success and deeper learning. Now in designing activities, assignments, or considering appropriate feedback to students, faculty can include the discovery of and analysis of mistakes as important to learning. Finally, mindset science encourages faculty to foster a sense of belonging to the academic and institutional community. Finally, mindset encourages faculty to clarify with students the purpose of a course and its assignments.

Focusing on the learners—what their preconceptions are, how they have learned to learn previously, and what sociocultural and gender identities they possess—enables a plethora of design opportunities. The mindset lexicon enriches the focus on the learners in the classroom by offering additional complex concepts to incorporate.

Inclusive teaching strategies offer exciting developments for engaging students to learn course and disciplinary content. In many courses, the faculty's choice of experts and authorities can be broadened. Small group work offers many opportunities for students to identify and appreciate opposing points of view, areas of cultural difference, and emerging recognition of implicit bias. In fact, there are four major areas—course content, faculty-student interaction, student interaction, and instructional practices themselves—that can bring about slight and even major modifications of an existing course in ways that strongly spark student interest and connection to the course and the class members of the course.

Much learning occurs within the classroom, particularly as the classroom minutes are used to address major questions, problems, or challenges that students have. In-class activities can include traditional evidence-based practices such as the daily quiz, or think-pair-share, the use of the pause, or even the rhetorical question. Eric Mazur's use of peer teaching has grown tremendously as has student facilitation of class discussion.

The flipped classroom allows for talking time to be less about conveying course information per se and more about moving students to deeper applications and understanding. In this kind of classroom, paired and group work become vehicles for peer explanation, technology becomes another vehicle to address specific questions and challenges, and individual/group presentations become opportunities for students to informally/or formally be present in ways that mere sitting and listening precluded.

Some courses can employ a more comprehensive structure such as Team-Based Learning which can use many of the minutes of the class every day, or nearly every day. A pedagogy like Reacting to the Past—a game script and individual roles for student to play—can also become the course idea that governs how time is dedicated during class minutes.

The online or hybrid classroom has changed dramatically for the better since the early days of the mail-in correspondence courses. Communication can be synchronous or asynchronous now, and the treasure trove of technologies has refined the meanings of engagement for online, hybrid, and face-to-face classes. Simulations, games, virtual worlds, videos, and such tools as discussion boards, have made these modalities potentially as engaging as the potential for learning in face-to-face classes. Now, faculty are more limited by lack of training with the technology than capability of the technology.

These several examples may suffice to demonstrate that class minutes are as rich a source of learning as any, so integrating the pedagogy and the content of the course with attention to class minutes is vital. With that acknowledged, the deepest, most abiding, learning occurs outside the classroom in a variety of contexts that employ one or more of the eleven High-Impact Practices (HIPS).[4]

When done well, a HIP can place students in situations where they can rely on course content, apply that content, and reflect on what they have learned on many levels. The Eight Essential Elements of a High-Impact Practice, when seriously applied to one's course, can help ensure that the individual High-Impact Practice will involve deep and lifelong learning for students.[5]

Thus far, the teaching moves have focused on what faculty can do to provide a rich, complex learning environment. Student assignments, much like the experiential High-Impact Practices, when well designed, call for students to apply and upon reflection to integrate course materials. To undertake a research project, to complete multiple in-depth writing assignments that can involve multiple drafts, to conduct experiments, to present one's findings—all of these and more are assignments that challenge students to follow protocol, to apply disciplinary methods, and to analyze results, at a high level.

Taken as self-evidently clear in the past, now it is understood much more clearly that the way that assignments are rhetorically formed has a lot to do with the learning of students. The work of Mary-Ann Winkelmas and her invaluable contribution of Transparency in Learning and Teaching (TiLT) have given faculty the way to render assignments both simpler in a way and certainly more understandable for students.[6] To "Tilt" an assignment, the faculty can take an old assignment, pare down the many directions about length, font type, description of genre, and the like and simply write the Purpose of the assignment in one or two sentences. Then, revise the pages of description to direct, brief statements of Tasks the student will complete to be successful. And finally, a third brief statement of Criteria for evaluation is given. How will students be evaluated in this assignment? TiLT workshops are much in demand, because getting into the actual words on the page about an existing assignment into the three parts of a Tilted assignment takes practice.

As with many of the previous advances affecting course design, so it is with assessment of learning. A single cumulative multiple-choice exam that this author took in first year political science is gratefully a relic of the past. Assessment exists to discern the learning of students, not simply to give faculty something to put on a semester grade report. Effective assessment moves from low stakes to high stakes work, offers frequent and meaningful feedback (now, available in different modalities), and evaluates course products that are meaningful instances of work in the discipline or related to applications of course content. Rubrics (also TiLT-ed) are vital parts of this assessment work.

Courses that integrate many of the engaged pedagogies cited here may become what Ken Bain has called Super Courses, which are those courses that have multiple key strategies.[7] One may wonder whether a defining quality or the cumulative impact of multiple strengths make a course a superior learning experience for students. And the truth may be something of both, in many cases. A couple of course examples may demonstrate how many pedagogical areas can be deployed in an individual course.

Two Example Courses: Finding the Golden Thread

For those who are unfamiliar with them, American literature survey courses are just what the name suggests, a chronological readings course covering centuries of anthologized works. For a nonmajor, such a readings course can be not only unedifying, but also feel entirely irrelevant to important issues they face.

Redesigning a common American Literature survey course around the issues related to the Canon can fortunately thread the readings, class discussion, and student research projects with a central motivation for students. Of course, having students engaged in an issue within the discipline as early as possible is desirable, but the connection to the motivation and the connection to the students are vital and work like this.

Students engage with multiple related questions such as what makes a good book a great one, how does a canon form, or is there a single canon or multiple canons, or should we have a canon at all? These broad questions are slowly addressed by the materials the class discussion generates, with the help of several materials placed on library reserve (anthologies going back to the 1920s, critical works on canon scholarship, collections of essays on the critical debate involving the canon, and multimedia recordings of conversation on the questions).

Their essays and research projects bring seemingly unrelated outside works into the discussion as students advocate that a favorite beloved book be included by our criteria for greatness. Research projects are written and also presented, and every position on the spectrum is honored when supported by good argument and evidence.

Another example of how the mix of engagement strategies can vary is designing a Special Topics Writing Intensive course organized around the question of What is Tragedy? This course does not involve the challenge of creating a way to organize and connect two hundred years of literature. Rather, the What is Tragedy course involves addressing a central question and a host of related questions that begin with the genre of Tragedy as an art form.

This big question, also integral to disciplinary investigation into genre, for one thing, invited all sorts of comparisons to fiction, drama, and television shows. Students' essays and research projects ranged across the genres, the media, and classical to modern definitions of the term Tragedy. From Aristotle to American Tragedy, students tend to intensely explore definitions, examples, essays, and critical positions in order to produce a satisfying response to the big question of the course.

Although each of these courses was composed of very different content and driven by a unique central question, some pedagogical practices remained the same: student motivation was regularly gauged in required one-on-one conferences for essays and the research project, every written assignment could be developed over multiple drafts, daily quizzes encouraged students to stay up with the assigned work in order to earn easy quiz points, student identity was engaged in the range of research topics and essay topics.

In both courses, success began early by asking students simply to read and take factual quizzes on the readings. Complexity built up over time as the class built a list of American Literature Issues through class discussion. Assignments also moved from simple and brief to longer papers with secondary sources.

Types of assessment of student learning included the following: Minute Paper, Low Stakes writing each day, swap and grade, daily quizzes, multiple drafts of every essay, research project built incrementally over the last six weeks of the semester, and multiple stages with assessments at each stage.

These two courses are similar in fundamental ways to all of the writing courses offered over ten years at Oxford College of Emory University in that students were invited to add readings and also to focus on others that the class did not undertake, thus modifying the syllabus in a very dynamic way.

Student work was treated in a similar way, offering students choices of topics and multiple draft opportunities for each writing assignment. Each course included a research project, another feature that opened conversation about ways to connect course materials to an area of interest for each student. Every research project was also presented in class, so students could create individual or group presentations, panels, and use a number of technologies in the presentation.

Thus, the combined impact of many different course elements all integrated well and joined to an overarching idea that runs through the entire course— this is the way to create excellent learning opportunities for all students.

When a faculty development expert works with faculty to fashion their own pedagogy involving the key elements and producing fantastic courses of their own, it is a rewarding, even humbling, experience. One course, which resulted from such a collaboration, was a Spanish language class using photographs to deconstruct stereotypes as depicted in the photos. Another course idea was an anthropology course which involved constructing a board game to explore social customs and practices. A Latin class employed team-based learning to interpret classical Latin passages. Each of these ideas provided the pedagogy and the disciplinary structure for the course, and in some cases perhaps the foundation of the academic inquiry for the course. There are simply too many great courses to mention.

A different way to think of excellent courses, however, is to distill the multiple key qualities they tend to possess. Ken Bain offers almost twenty discrete traits as a comprehensive list of traits that tend to emerge in clusters of several traits at a time.[8] A comprehensive list such as this is not meant to be a checklist, but a list of possible features to consult as a great course is being built.

So whether one begins with an overarching idea and retains the best practices in other key elements that are already employed, or builds a course by reflecting on a number of good possibilities, one thing is certain—abiding reflection and examination of courses should be continuous. A great course is not set or static.

MULTIPLE POINTS OF ENTRY

A class activity, game, or discussion, a difficult conversation, an engaging assignment or research project, an out of class experience within a High-Impact Practice in service learning or an internship—all of these elements offer points of entry for students.

A connection with a student in conference or in the hall can provide the relational spark that motivates and creates belonging. The work of Daniel Chambliss emphasizes that relationships are often precursors to vital learning and serve as motivation for remaining and working successfully across the degree pathway.[9] More recently, the book by Peter Felten and Leo M. Lambert also underscores the influence of relationships.[10]

In some very real ways, the design, the practices, and the behaviors make the content come to life and become more memorable, more deeply acquired. Hence, the clever and profound "teaching moves" may not be seen as much as felt by students as the activities foster belonging, interest, connection, and learning. It becomes natural.

This book proposes a way of creating learning experiences, and this chapter has presented the nuts and bolts of this process. Many faculty have undertaken the process, so one can only imagine what learning will happen once all faculty have redesigned their courses for student learning.

NOTES

1. Gerald Graff and Cathy Birkenstein, *They Say / I Say: The Moves That Matter in Academic Writing* (New York: Norton Press, 2014).

2. Jeffery Galle and Denise P. Domizi, eds., *Faculty Learning Communities: Chancellor's Learning Communities for Student Success* (Lanham, MD: Rowman & Littlefield, 2021) and *Campus Conversations: Student Success Pedagogies in Practice* (Lanham, MD: Rowman & Littlefield, 2021).

3. L. Dee Fink, *Creating Significant Learning Experiences: An Integrated Approach to Designing College Courses* (San Francisco: Jossey-Bass, 2003).

4. Much more information, examples, and assessment materials on HIPS are here: https://www.aacu.org/trending-topics/high-impact.

5. High-Impact Practices themselves do not guarantee successful learning. The evidence shows that students who experience the HIPS done well learn deeply. The 8 Key Elements acts to support HIPS done well: chrome-extension://efaidnbmnnni bpcajpcglclefindmkaj/http://ts3.nashonline.org/wp-content/uploads/2018/04/AACU -LEAP-High-Impact-Practice-Characteristics.pdf.

6. Examples of and research on TiLT are here: https://tilthighered.com/.

7. Ken Bain, *Super Courses: The Future of Teaching and Learning* (Princeton: Princeton University Press, 2021).

8. The individual components are like individual pedagogies or contexts for student learning in *Super Courses*, pp. 31–34. Paraphrasing Bain's list for our own use looks something like the following: the course focuses on big questions and what work it requires to answer them; students are given multiple occasions to learn before grading applies, and/or at the least grading is scaled; students collaborate on projects; hypothesizing with examination of potential causes is employed; faculty discern existing paradigms that students are using; courses explore the weaknesses of current

paradigms; faculty develop student ownership of their learning, their projects, and their responsibility for learning; faculty offer all types of support as needed (emotional, intellectual, physical); faculty develop fair, transparent, equitable grading, and underscore effort matters; faculty reward multiple attempts; faculty focus on growth mindset qualitiesparticularly that intelligence is flexible and can grow; faculty focus on student belief that they can learn and that the teacher is not there to identify "winners/losers"; faculty employ multiple ways to include diverse cultures, genders, and ways of learning: diversity prized; faculty through course work have them doing the discipline from the start; faculty focus on ways to learn inductively, not only deductively; and faculty employ other disciplines in the course to address key questions, inquiry, and research.

9. See Daniel F. Chambliss and Christopher G. Takacs, *How College Works* (Cambridge, MA: Harvard University Press, 2014). "Person-to-person relationships are fundamental at every stage—before, during, and after the core learning activities of college," p. 4. And, "The pervasive influence of relationships suggests that a college—at least insofar as it offers real benefits—is less a collection of programs than a gathering of people," p. 5.

10. Peter Felten and Leo M. Lambert, *Relationship-Rich Education* (Baltimore: Johns Hopkins Press, 2020), 85.

For building personal connections, Felten suggests four things: learning names of students, returning early assignments with formative feedback, signaling to struggling students that rigor and success are possible, meeting individually with students one on one for 10–15 minutes.

Chapter 2

Designing a "Cool Class" for All Modalities

Jim Fatzinger

Today's classroom, an active "learning laboratory," is comprised of multiple generations of teachers and learners including baby boomers, Generation X, millennials, and Generation Z.[1] Each student has his/her own preference for content delivery, communication, and historical milestones. Instructors also should consider the perspective that they bring to the classroom as well as that of the learners. Every course is different, varying not only with its modality, but its instructor, enrollment, learners' preexisting understanding, and experience.

Quality course design is then an iterative process rather than a static process, ever-evolving in approaches to pedagogy, application of content, and ongoing assessment of learning. Recognition that the gap in technologies utilized in the classroom and those utilized in industry has narrowed, is also important.

Developing a "Cool Class" begins with an interest in the learner and requires intentionality. When considering Wiggins and McTighe's principles of "Backward Design,"[2] for example, the authors relate: "Teachers are designers. An essential act of our profession is crafting our curriculum and learning experiences to meeting specific purposes."

This chapter, based on a BUS306 Essential of Supply Chain Management course which I designed at Eastern Kentucky University (EKU), was later selected by EKU's Faculty Center for Teaching and Learning as a "Cool Class" feature because of the course's quality design and implementation. Ideas presented in this chapter are coupled with theory and student feedback, providing opportunities for application and reflection. Audiences include those designing, assessing, and evaluating courses. "Lessons learned" may be applied to a variety of technology platforms and settings including higher education, government, non-profits, and industries.

BUS306, Essentials of Supply Chain Management, explores the strategic management of operations and the supply chain with the overall objective of global optimization. Course topics include strategic planning, forecasting, quality, logistics, project management, and inventory management. The application of the course description to the experience of the instructor, pacing of the course content, the progression of the learners in their collegiate progression, and the experience of the learners enrolled, provides an opportunity for sparking interest as well as creating a positive first impression for the learner. Initial course design should be intentional, engaging, conscientious of course time, and offer an opportunity for the sharing of common experiences with the curriculum by both the instructor and the learner. It's essential to create an environment where those new to the topic also feel comfortable.

To design my BUS306 Essentials of Supply Chain Management course, I began by:

1. Revisiting the course description.

    Course descriptions in a curriculum, at times, lag behind key concepts evolving in the business environment, and in revisiting the course description, goals, and learning outcomes, opportunities incorporating the latest avant-garde business applications arise. While some applications may be fads, others may represent current/feature industry trends and should be considered in context. Current events also offer opportunities for curriculum design, redesign, student engagement, and critical assessment.

2. Enriching the content of the course by bringing in industry leaders and employers.

    Industry leader perspectives, current articles, and/or videos from those in the field, both in agreement and contradiction with the curriculum, allow for critical thinking while enabling students to make connections between key course concepts and industry, thus promoting students' understanding.

    My BUS306 course curriculum also was greatly enhanced with the addition of corporate facilitators. In the first half of the course, the Corporate Operations Manager of Kentucky's own "Big Ass Fans" worked with various course topics on an on-going basis, including operations, supply chain, competitiveness, strategy, productivity, and forecasting. This corporate leader also included a video which enhanced course curriculum, and he worked one-on-one with students to provide feedback on assignments. At the conclusion of the first half of the course, he invited students to tour the corporate facility. Assessments supported student learning outcomes on an on-going basis.

In the second half of the course, students learned from an industry leader at Kentucky's own Lexington Legends, a hospitality company founded in 2001, who provided a video on course topics related to services. Assessments included a summative culminating evaluation. Thus, BUS306 has evolved over time based on student feedback, evaluation, and instructor knowledge.

3. Considering the progression of the learners in their collegiate experience (including course prerequisites).

    To ensure that a course is both academically rigorous and incorporates what the students already know, the instructor needs to know what the prerequisites are.

4. Assessing successes and opportunities for improvement from previous semesters by considering my student and peer faculty evaluations.

    It is also essential for the instructor to know which techniques and teaching strategies that he/she used helped previous students learn the most—and what did not.

5. Reviewing and developing course goals.

    Having a clear set of learning goals helps the instructor design the course with intention.

6. When appropriate, a theme for a course can be developed. With over a decade of teaching experience, national presentations, and lectures at institutions including Brown University, Clemson University, Vanderbilt University, the United States Air Force Academy, and University of Georgia, I have learned from those in attendance as well as shared experiences. Generally, presentations include an overarching theme followed by information that supports the theme. The BUS306 course also is themed—around excerpts from Charlie Chaplain's silent film, *Modern Times*. It is ironic that the film was silent and produced in 1936 inside a simulated manufacturing facility This initial course theme emphasizes how supply chain impacts all areas of "modern times."

    The course's theming of the content around Charlie Chaplain's 1936 silent film *Modern Times* illustrates fundamental concepts, challenges learner perceptions, and by the conclusion of the course, provides applications for learners in their daily lives.

7. Engaging learners prior to the start of the semester. In designing the BUS306 course, students selected the order of the topics covered by prioritizing their interests in a survey prior to the semester start. Here's how:

a. One week prior to the start of the course, students could prioritize the lessons in the course with their collective interests, and then the course content timeline was modified to reflect learner interest.

b. Once students have responded with their prioritization, I then selected elements of the feedback from the learners and revised the syllabus and course design to include the relevant parts from the student feedback.

After the initial syllabus and learning plan are developed, pre-course student feedback and learner experience allow for the on-going enrichment of curriculum. As the course progresses, modifications unique to each offering may be made maximizing student engagement and ensuring learning outcomes are achieved. My approach to developing this BUS306 course occurred over several iterations and were well-received by students. Selected student feedback provided additional opportunities for reflection and ultimately, the "cool class" feature. The approaches outlined in this article promote audience engagement, provide innovative, avant-garde, pedagogical application, and encourage incorporating student feedback within the uniqueness of each course offering.

As one student suggested in the evaluation: "I find this teaching style to work very well with how I learn and because of this I feel as if I have actually learned about operations management."

NOTES

1. R. Fry, "Millennials are the largest generation in the U.S. labor force," *Pew Research Center,* 2018; L. Hillery and N. Dan-Bergman, "How Graduate Schools Must Change Their Approach inPursuit of Gen Z," PowerPoint Slides, *AACSB Insights Research Roundup by AACSBStaff, "Is Higher Ed Ready for Gen Z?"* May 2022, https://www.aacsb.edu/insights/articles/2022/05/research-roundup-may-2022.

2. Grant Wiggins and Jay McTighe, *Understanding by Design* (New York: Association for Supervision and Curriculum Development, 2005).

REFERENCES

Fry, R. "Millennials are the largest generation in the U.S. labor force." Pew Research Center, 2018.

Hillery, L. and N. Dan-Bergman. "How Graduate Schools Must Change Their Approach in Pursuit of Gen Z." PowerPoint Slides. *AACSB Insights Research Roundup by AACSBStaff: "Is Higher Ed Ready for Gen Z?"* May 2022. https://www.aacsb.edu/insights/articles/2022/05/research-roundup-may-2022

Wiggins, Grant and Jay McTighe. *Understanding by Design.* New York: Association for Supervision and Curriculum Development, 2005.

Chapter 3

Strategizing "Failure"

Found Texts, Inquiry, and Building New Mental Models

Rebecca L. Harrison

When I attended my first pedagogy conference on inquiry-based practices well over a decade ago, I had to quickly reckon with one humbling truth: what I thought were high-impact practices in my classrooms were not actually leading students to developing deep, portable skills. I simply did not understand enough about *how* students learn, why their mental modes change slowly, and how to implement a more developmentally informed view of learning in my literature curriculums.

Ken Bain, acclaimed author of *What the Best College Teachers Do*, changed that with a keynote focused on the necessity of understanding existing student mental paradigms and, more to the point, the instructional potency of drawing them into question. His talk, and the small experiential group session that followed, incited a long and ever-evolving study of inquiry methods—practices that center "construction" as equally important as traditional notions of discipline "coverage"—that drive both how I prepare for and conduct class.

One of the most effective high-impact practices that I regularly deploy as a beginning exercise in all of my classes is the expectation failure. As Bain describes, expectation failures are generated when teachers create situations wherein students' existing "mental model[s]," the ways of thinking that they bring to the classroom, "will not help them explain or do something" (28).

Such activities are strategically structured to invest students in the work— so that they care their existing paradigms fail—and to build both an intrinsic desire to contend with complex problems and grow new ways of thinking. They generally end with meaningful reflective spaces where students recognize and have conversations about the implications of the exercise for themselves and for the larger goals of the course. Beginning my courses with a robust "Found Text" exercise squarely centering the expectation failure, thus, allows my students to "try their own thinking, come up short, receive feedback, and try again" while also exposing them to essential discipline concepts. [1]

STAGING THE INVESTIGATION

The class is divided into small groups of no more than five students each, and the students are presented with the following situation. They represent a team of expert explorers who have excavated a room prophesized to hold the key to help them solve, think through, or make sense of some event, tragedy, or human story that they are concerned with. The only object they find in the room, however, is an envelope containing six torn pieces of a written text that they do not recognize. [2] They must use their combined expertise to put the pieces of writing together again by making sense of the text and then draw conclusions about its historical context and meaning (potential period, genre, author and their positionality, theme, audience, etc.).[3]

The student teams then open their envelopes, closely examine the six pieces of the found text, and spend twenty-minutes on the task. In a decade of using the exercise, the same group pattern occurs. They first try to literally reconstruct the six pieces of paper based on their visual observations as they appear like a puzzle that can be reassembled; in actuality, the edges have been randomized and do not fit together. When that fails, they move on to study-ing the actual text and, particularly, its rhetorical structures, looking for other patterns they can identify to guide both its literal reconstructions and their discussion of its meaning and historicity.

Groups are then asked to share their findings, and how they derived at those conclusions based on textual evidence. They know up front that each team will have the opportunity to either agree with or counter any previous team's assertions. As the designated scribe and mediator, I write the first group's findings on the white board using a black Expo marker. I then select another group and give them the opportunity to agree or disagree with any facet of team one's findings based on either additional textual evidence or a different interpretation of the evidence already presented. Agreements are noted with a green Expo marker, and disagreements are noted in red. This process continues until all groups have reported out and a complex debate evolves on the board. Before we move on, groups are given the opportunity to confer and modify, if deemed necessary, any of their original conclusions based on the full class discussion.[4]

Finally, I read the found text pieces in the correct order and reveal its full contextual information. The students then spend the final segment of class reflecting deeply on the activity, the hypotheses they made about the text, and what those assumptions reveal about themselves, their biases, their modes of thinking, and their reading practices. Before they leave, I assign the full found text for the next class period.[5]

Found Texts: A Sample

I often use a robust section from William Apess's "An Indian's Looking Glass for the White Man" (1833), a text most of my students have not been exposed to before (see figure 3.1).[6] They immediately seize upon the references to "black principles," "black inconsistency," and "skin" contained in the six fragments and polarize social justice in America as a white/black binary in their thinking about the case study. Almost without exception, by the end of the debate period, they place the piece in the civil rights era most likely written by an African American preacher or politician. Thus, when the Apess reveal occurs, they have to reconsider and texture their thinking about race, history, and nation, and their own reading practices.[7]

While the found text exercise leads to a discipline focused discussion in the next class session, its use during our first content-based class period of the term centers them, the students, as the first "text" our course considers. The exercise changes their lenses in a way that helps them enter the material work of our class more quickly and in more critically nuanced ways. It also invests them in me and the intellectual investigations to come.

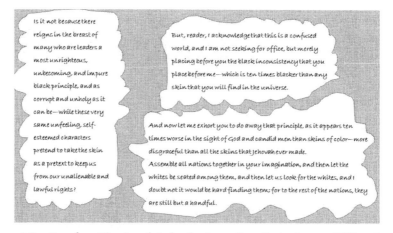

Is it not because there reigns in the breast of many who are leaders a most unrighteous, unbecoming, and impure black principle, and as corrupt and unholy as it can be—while these very same unfeeling, self-esteemed characters pretend to take the skin as a pretext to keep us from our unalienable and lawful rights?

But, reader, I acknowledge that this is a confused world, and I am not seeking for office, but merely placing before you the black inconsistency that you place before me—which is ten times blacker than any skin that you will find in the universe.

And now let me exhort you to do away that principle, as it appears ten times worse in the sight of God and candid men than skins of color—more disgraceful than all the skins that Jehovah ever made. Assemble all nations together in your imagination, and then let the whites be seated among them, and then let us look for the whites, and I doubt not it would be hard finding them; for to the rest of the nations, they are still but a handful.

Figure 3.1. Sample cutting template for the Apess Case Study. *Source: William Apess's "An Indian's Looking Glass for the White Man" (1833).*

NOTES

1. These quotes are from Bain, p. 28. Note: Jeff Galle introduced me to a variation of this exercise at the 2010 Institute for Pedagogy in the Liberal Arts. My iteration deploys a two-part expectation failure, a second layer of inquiry, and a class debate that leads out to our first literary unit. These modifications follow the seven unifying principles Ken Bain outlines for successfully conducting class (pp. 98–134). The exercise is fully distillable, across subject and level, by simply substituting the found text with one appropriate for the goals of the course.

2. The text selection is carefully curated each term for each course's outcomes and with what I know about my students' learning patterns and their cultural and reading biases. Texts may also be images or other artifacts.

3. In a full format inquiry class, what some scholars refer to as open inquiry, I would have them determine what questions need asking of the text rather than providing the areas and elements of literary history to consider.

4. This element of the activity takes approximately thirty minutes.

5. In my pedagogy courses, they also reflect on the exercise's design as future educators.

6. William Apess was a Native American intellectual, advocate, and preacher from the nineteenth century.

7. Apess is just one example from my archive of found texts; selections must be regularly rotated to maintain effectiveness.

REFERENCES

Apess, W. *On our own ground: the complete writings of William Apess, a Pequot.* Amherst: University of Massachusetts Press, 1992.

Bain, K. *What the best college teachers do.* Cambridge, MA: Harvard University Press, 2004.

Chapter 4

Using Growth Mindset to Facilitate Belonging in First Year Writing

Julie Kozee

My first-year writing classes are gateway courses. Students in the liminal sequence of freshman composition often feel Othered, left outside the college community, due to not being fully prepared for the courses they are now facing. Some have returned to school after a long hiatus, others are working full-time or caring for a family, and some are recent high school graduates who weren't fully engaged during their K–12 years. These students transition from Other to member of the college community in composition courses through growth mindset, developed by psychologist Carol Dweck. In fact, teaching growth mindset benefits all students, both those who are insecure about their abilities and those who are high achieving, especially when they struggle and do not know what to do.

WHAT IS THE ASSIGNMENT

Students write a short "growth mindset" essay early in the semester. In this assignment, they write a metacognitive narrative that defines their current mindset about writing and describes strategies that they can use to obtain or maintain a growth mindset in the class. They must explain how each strategy will help them develop or strengthen a growth mindset.

HOW DOES IT WORK

Prior to this essay assignment, students have learned about growth mindsets, fixed mindsets, and false growth mindset, so they feel confident in identifying the mindset they have toward academic writing. They have also learned strategies they can use to obtain a growth mindset, such as asking questions when they don't understand, using the tutorial and writing center services they have available to them, reaching out to their instructor for help either during office hours or via email, attending class every day, and more. We begin with an online discussion board, and everyone shares their current mindset toward academic writing. *Communitas* is created during these discussions, which allows students to feel more comfortable sharing their insecurities in their "growth mindset" essays. The essays are first graded as rough drafts, with feedforward language used on a detailed rubric. Students revise their essays and resubmit for a final grade, putting in practice the growth mindset strategies described in their drafts.

WHO BENEFITS

Through this assignment, students learn the strategies needed to enter the college community with a full sense of belonging because they are now prepared for the challenges ahead (figures 4.1 and 4.2). Additionally, DFW rates trend downward, and ABC grades trend upward in a class where students have been explicitly taught growth mindset (table 4.1). As instructors, we are able to meaningfully connect with our students, demonstrating our own growth mindset toward them and their abilities through essay feedback and discussions. The college benefits from increased retention rates: students who feel like they belong are more likely to engage in campus activities, interact with their faculty, and graduate.

Table 4.1.

	DFW % DROP	DF RATE % DROP	ABC RATE % INCREASE
FALL 2017–FALL 2018	20.3	21	13.3
FALL 2017–FALL 2021	25.4	28.15	13.9

Change in DFW rates for Dr. Kozee. Improvement in DFW, DF, and ABC rates in J. Kozee's ENGL 1101 classes from first fall semester growth mindset assignment was used to second fall semester it was used, and improvement in DFW, DF, and ABC rates in J. Kozee's ENGL 1101 classes from first fall semester growth mindset assignment was used to most recent fall semester it was used. Statistics provided by the Dean of Institutional Effectiveness and Strategic Initiatives at Georgia Highlands College. *Source: IR Office, Georgia Highlands College.*

I found the first assignment of this course, a reading on psychologist Carol Dweck's concept of growth and fixed mindsets, to be exciting and compelling, causing me to think in different and unexpected ways. It represented for me, as stated by Dweck, "what we psychologists call an Aha! experience" (Dweck 5). It became clear to me that I was coming into this course with a very fixed mindset, which included false preconceptions and low expectations, and that I was being challenged to look at things quite differently, and to be much more engaged. Approaching the course, I had been irritated that it was a requirement, as I already hold a bachelor's degree from another college. Learning the value of a growth mindset has reshaped my perspective on the opportunity to learn which this course represents. In this essay I will provide

Figure 4.1. Student Reflective Essay quote. Portion of Student Reflective Essay (unpublished). *Source: Author.*

Having a growth mind-set for this aspect of my life will lead me into success. I won't have these self-doubts. I will work harder. If I were do adopt a growth mind-set in my calculus class, that would mean, I will not look at failure as, "I am stupid" instead I'll look at the failure as a learning experience for me to work harder and seek out additional help. With a growth mind-set my inner thoughts would be, " It's okay if I fail, I just need to know what I did wrong so I won't make that same mistake" or, " I can do anything I put my mind to" or even, " My intelligence will grow as long as I do, I will pass this class!"

There will be a lot of changes for me to adopt this growth mind-set for this aspect of my life. I will need to ultimately change the way I think. I cannot sit in class quiet because I'm

Figure 4.2. Student Reflective Essay quote. Portion of Student Reflective Essay (unpublished). *Source: Author.*

CONCLUSION

Taking a small amount of time at the beginning of the semester to engage with our students and share growth mindset strategies, which are essential to their success, gives our students innumerable advantages. While I have only attempted this assignment in my composition classes, it lends itself nicely to other gateway courses, such as the chemistry course my non-native English-speaking female student was struggling with in figure 4.2, or the redundant courses my non-trad male student was annoyed with in figure 4.1. While professors across the disciplines might not wish to deliver the assignment in this mode, an essay, there are many other ways to teach and then practice growth mindset: in-depth discussion boards, class discussions (for synchronous classes), working in small groups and then sharing out to the class, or "exit tickets" from James Lang's *Small Teaching*. It could even be incorporated as part of the course policy; for example, the "second chances" policy, which allows students to request another chance at a failed attempt, but they first have to reflect on their mistakes and explain the strategies they will use in their second chance at success. This can be a short, written assignment, a fill-in-the blanks on a pre-made form, or a short conversation with the professor during office hours. Overall, this is a relatively easy lesson to teach and assignment to give and grade, especially in a composition class. As professors, we just need to use our creativity to adopt work across disciplines to make use of it in our courses. Most of us are fortunate to have instructional designers at our institution, and they can help us adapt curriculum, create new curriculum, and use new and/or adapted curriculum most effectively.

REFERENCES

Dweck, C. S. (2006). Mindset: The new psychology of success. Random House.
Lang, J. (2016). Small teaching: Everyday lessons from the science of learning. San
    Francisco: Jossey-Bass.

Chapter 5

How Focusing on Learning from Mistakes Facilitated Learning in Calculus Class

Veena Paliwal

I taught two sections of calculus in fall 2021. Students' understanding was examined by their performance in the three exams covering different topics from the syllabus (exam 1: limits and derivatives; exam 2: applications of derivatives, and exam 3: antiderivatives). Each exam was scheduled every fifth week of the semester. Research has shown that mathematical concepts are interrelated and build on the understanding of previous concepts.[1]

It was crucial that the students have a thorough understanding of derivatives (a topic covered in exam 1) to learn the material and be successful in upcoming next exams. Exam 1 results indicated that most students lacked deep understanding of the material and it was evident that this would hamper their performance in the upcoming exams.

THE PROJECT

In my classes, I often highlighted the importance of growth mindset—belief that an individual's most basic abilities can be developed through dedication and hard work—brains and talent are just the starting point. One of the positive outcomes of having growth mindset is viewing mistakes as blessings and using them constructively as tools for learning.[2] To facilitate students in getting better scores for upcoming two exams, I decided to test an outcome of developing growth mindset that involves learning from mistakes.

Design

Experimental design was used where participants from class 1 served as the experimental group and received intervention on using mistakes as a learning tool along with the usual instruction. The other class served as the control group and received the usual classroom instruction.

Measures

Measures were follow up exams that evaluated immediate (exam 2) and delayed (exam 3) impact of the intervention. Participants also filled out a student engagement survey before and after the intervention.

Intervention

Both classes received step-by-step solutions to the twenty-five problems from exam 1. Participants from class 1 participated in literature discussion about the importance of mistakes (Boaler, 2022) in mathematics and were, then, asked to identify their mistakes by comparing their answers with the answer key from exam 1. Students' self-evaluation of their performance helped in identifying the level of understanding that students have attained about particular mathematical concepts and further led to categorize mistakes as: numerical (mostly algebraic) and conceptual (lacking concepts understanding).

HOW MISTAKES HELPED WITH MY INSTRUCTION

In weeks 6–15 of the semester, I adopted a different instructional technique for class 1 that involved working on correcting possible mistakes on new topics that were introduced in the class. This involved: revisiting the mistakes based on the analysis of students' self-reported mistakes from exam 1, engaging students in collaborative work for identifying the source of wrong solutions and working on a strategy to correct them, and rephrasing steps involved in computations by providing algebraic justification and connecting them with students' existing knowledge.

HOW IT HELPED MY STUDENTS

The intervention was successful in improving participants' performance as revealed by the results of the three exams. There was no significant difference between the experimental group and the control group in exam 1

$(t(57) = 0.02, p = 0.4)$. However, the experimental participants performed significantly better than the control participants in exam 2 $(t(57) = 1.92, p = .03)$ and exam 3 $(t(57) = 2.03, p = 0.03)$. Students' average score on the engagement survey revealed experimental participants' engagement improved, $t(28) = 17.81, p < 0.01$, between pre-survey and post-survey. There was not a significant improvement in the student engagement for the control group participants, $t(29) = 1.19, p = 0.12$.

SIGNIFICANCE

The findings of the study highlight the importance of using mistakes as a learning tool. Growth Mindset perspective of mistakes is critical to the mathematics classrooms, and education in general, and it can be a tool to redefine pedagogical practices to improve teaching and learning outcomes and practices.

NOTES

1. Bourbaki, 1950; Batanero, & Díaz, 2007.
2. Boaler, 2016; Mueller & Dweck, 1998; Sun, 2015.

REFERENCES

Batanero, C., & Díaz, C. The meaning and understanding of mathematics. In *Philosophical dimensions in mathematics education* (pp. 107–127). Boston, MA: Springer, 2007.

Boaler, J. *Mathematical mindsets: Unleashing students' potential through creative mathematics*. Hoboken: Wiley & Sons, 2022.

Bourbaki, N. (1950). The architecture of mathematics. *The American Mathematical Monthly, 57*(4), 221–232.

Mueller, C. M., & Dweck, C. S. (1998). Praise for intelligence can undermine children's motivation and performance. *Journal of Personality and Social Psychology, 75*(1), 33.

Sun, K. L. (2015). *There's no limit: Mathematics teaching for a growth mindset*. Stanford University.

Chapter 6

Won't You Be My Neighbor?

A Learning Community Experiment

Lindsay Bailey, Shane Toepfer, and Laura Ng

On our small, 2,500 student commuter campus, we have a two-year mission to help students transition to either a larger campus at the University of North Georgia or another system school. The biggest obstacles we face as a commuter campus in a larger, five-campus university are students who feel isolated and are unaware of available resources, making them less able to make social connections. This disconnectedness results in students lacking a sense of belonging on campus,[1] which is one of the most important factors of student persistence and wellbeing.[2] We designed a proactive intervention strategy to support learning and engage students.

WHAT DID WE DO?

Our learning community was meant to be a nexus of best practices from student involvement and academic pedagogy. We took a page from Dr. Robert Nash's *Crossover Pedagogy* and developed the course with a partner who is an expert in student development. Service learning helps students connect academic disciplines and real-life issues.[3] Student involvement provided a framework on student development and engagement that scaffolded the classroom design.

We emphasized community. We provided a common media experience early in the semester by watching *Won't You Be My Neighbor*. We highlighted a key question from the documentary, which described a "neighborhood" as a space that protected you when you were feeling unsafe, and asked students to reflect on whether UNG operated as this sort of neighborhood. This emphasis on neighborhood and community, and how we hope to make positive contributions to these communities, guided course projects.

The semester concluded with a service learning project where students thought about ways to address communities' issues. They worked with community partners, such as Keep Athens Clarke County Beautiful and the Northeast Georgia Food Bank, and attempted to improve the conditions of their communities. Many projects centered on the UNG community and included attempts to educate fellow students about issues such as screen time, money management, and sexual assault, all issues that were significant to our students. We also implemented a co-curricular "badge" assignment to encourage our students to think about UNG as their community. Students earned their badges by meeting with advisors, attending club meetings, and engaging in services on campus.

HOW DID STUDENTS BENEFIT?

Our learning community emphasized the importance of community, connection, and our ability to create change. In a survey, a majority of students reported an increase in their level of academic and social confidence. They felt less anxious participating in discussions, were more comfortable engaging with people, and realized the supportive benefits of community. Our data, while problematized by the pandemic, indicates that our learning community helped students feel more connected to each other and to UNG.

HOW DID INSTRUCTORS BENEFIT?

We increased our foundational knowledge of each other's disciplines and students' lives. We learned about student development theory, developing a sense of belonging, facilitating class discussions, and adjusting the course structure for pace. We found a lovely crossover between academic disciplines. Learning in front of students gave us a chance to model ways to disagree and find compromise. We learned about our students' concerns for their communities, jobs, families, and future careers. On an institutional level, the badge assignment from our class currently serves as a model for a larger pilot program at UNG. It is in the pilot stage with fifteen paired classes that are supported with student involvement content as a part of the educational experience. UNG has plans to extend the program to other campuses.

NOTES

1. Strayhorn, 2012.
2. Kissane & McLaren, 2006.
3. Eppler et al., 2011; Zhao & Kuh, 2004.

REFERENCES

Eppler, M. A., Ironsmith, M., Dingle, S. H., & Errickson, M. A. (2011). Benefits of service-learning for freshmen college students and elementary school children. *Journal of the Scholarship of Teaching and Learning, 11*(4), 102–115.

Kissane, M., & McLaren, S. (2006). Sense of belonging as a predictor of reasons for living in older adults. *Death Studies, 30*(3), 243–258. https://doi.org/10.1080/07481180500493401

Nash, R. (2016). *Crossover pedagogy: A rationale for a new teaching partnership between faculty and student affairs leaders on college campuses.* Information Age Publishing.

Strayhorn, T. L. (2012). *College students' sense of belonging: A key to educational success for all students.* New York, NY: Routledge.

Won't you be my neighbor. Directed by Morgan Neville, Tremolo Productions, 2018.

Zhao, C. & Kuh, G. (2004). Adding value: Learning communities and student engagement. *Research in Higher Education, 45,* 115–138. 10.1023/B:RIHE.00000 15692.88534.de

Chapter 7

Small Teaching Strategy
Connecting through the Circle

Molly Zhou

After learning about small teaching strategies introduced in James Lang's book *Small Teaching: Everyday Lessons from the Science of Learning*, I focused on the connecting strategy, innovated it, and implemented it in the education foundation course Exploring Social Cultural Perspectives in Education through the Circle. As a small strategy, the Circle promotes learning community and equity (Reflection Circle Guide, 2022). The Circle symbolizes eternity, non-hierarchy, and the continuum. In the Circle, students see each other face to face. There are no beginning and ending. In Exploring Social Cultural Perspectives in Education course, students experience the Circle activity for about 10–15 minutes at the beginning, in the middle, or at the end of the class session several times in the course each semester.

In the beginning of the class session, the Circle helps gather students' attention and signals to them that it is time to focus on class. As a beginning activity for that session, the Circle brings students to discuss what is learned in the past class and what is to be learned in the present class. The Circle activity helps connect students' prior knowledge and provides opportunities for me to scaffold the class session. For some students who may be lacking, the Circle activity bridges the learning gap for them. For other students, the Circle is an opportunity to strengthen learned knowledge and connect that to new learning.

The Circle activity can be introduced in the middle of the class session as a strategy for engagement, knowledge development, scaffolding, and knowledge consolidation. The middle of the class is a good time to strengthen interaction with students. The change of classroom setting from row by row or from small group into a whole class learning circle refreshes students' mind. Moving the chairs around to form a big class circle gives students an opportunity to build the big picture of class community and to learn about others who they have not known yet.

The Circle at the end of the class is great for summary and reflection. According to Lang, the last few minutes of class are important and wasted if the instructor does not strategically make use of those few minutes to engage students in reinforcing their learning. In my Exploring Social Cultural Perspectives in Education course, I organize the class into a big class circle. These last few minutes at the end of class support students as they reflect on learning from the class period. It also helps build connections and refreshes knowledge for long term memory. In that sense, the Circle is deeply rooted in brain research and learning science.

It is worth pointing out that the magic of the Circle is the use of the talking piece. In my course, I used my personal cultural items of lived experiences to connect with students. During the Circle, the items get to be shared and passed around class. Through examining, touching, and feeling the talking pieces, students listen, connect, and understand the instructor more. In the Circle, stronger relationships are built between the instructor and the students and greater understanding for content is supported. To further help enrich connections through the classroom talking pieces, students bring their cultural items to serve as the talking piece for the Circle as well.

The experience of using the Circle to change learning in the classroom at the beginning, in the middle, and at the end of the class session was beneficial. Students enjoyed it, saying "I love it," "I can finally see the face of other students," and "We never did anything like this in other classes." Although originated in the field of criminal justice, the Circle is an interdisciplinary strategy (Davenport, 2018). Try this small but impactful teaching strategy to strengthen students' learning.

REFERENCES

Davenport, M. (2018). Using circle practice in the classroom. Retrieved from https://www.edutopia.org/article/using-circle-practice-classroom

Lang, J. (2016). *Small teaching: Everyday lessons from the science of learning*. San Francisco: Jossey-Bass.

Reflection Circle Guide. (2022). Retrieved from https://empatico.org/activity-plan/reflection-circle-guide

Chapter 8

What's in a Name?

Carl J. Gabrini

I noticed over time that my course evaluations were flat, and some student comments indicated a perception of distance between them and me. That bothered me because I care and want students to know I care. To improve my teaching and build better relationships with my students I decided to participate in the USG Chancellor's Learning Scholar Faculty Learning Communities (FLC). Through the FLC discussions, I became convicted about not knowing my students' names and not spending enough time learning them. Lang states "our names have tremendous power to capture our attention."[1]

What little research that exists on this topic supports the conclusion that students care about hearing their names used in class.[2] Armed with this information and my personal conviction I committed to making the effort to change.

In the Spring of 2022, I was assigned to teach three courses with a total of sixty-seven enrolled students. I reviewed the literature on techniques for learning names and decided to use a seating chart in my courses.[3] I shared with the students my struggle at learning names and asked for their help. I asked if they would select their own seats and remain in them for the first three weeks of the semester. I drew diagrams of the classrooms and wrote the students' names in their self-selected seating order. I studied the seating charts and used them to take attendance the first two weeks of class. By that time, I learned 90% of their names. By the end of the third week, I knew them all and no longer needed the charts to take attendance. I began using their names when they entered class, when I asked them questions, or if they asked me questions. I even made sure to call them by name whenever I saw them around campus.

As a result, I sensed a difference in my exchanges with students and in the classroom climate. However, to assess the impact of this small change I emailed my students asking them for feedback on my use of their names. What I learned in reading their responses is that my students appreciated my effort, felt valued and cared about, and felt more accountable.

One student noted they felt "more welcomed and at ease." Another stated they often feel they get drowned out in classes full of personalities and the fact I knew her name made her feel "heard." Yet another student commented it motivated them to work harder and increased her desire to do well. One student indicated they were often inclined to cut classes, but me knowing their name resulted in his decision to attend classes more often.

While the change may have been a minor one, the effect on my students was significant. It also supports the value of seeking opportunities to continuously improve my teaching through FLCs.

NOTES

1. Lang, *Distracted*, 107
2. Cooper et al., 2017; Lang, 2020, 108.
3. Syverud, 1993; Middendorf, 2002; Handy, 2008; Glenz, 2014; O'Brien et al., 2014; Cooper et al., 2017.

REFERENCES

Cooper, Katelyn M., Haney, Brian, Krieg, Anna, and Brownell, Sara E. (2017). What's in a Name? The Importance of Students Perceiving That an Instructor Knows Their Names in a High-Enrollment Biology Classroom. *CBE—Life Sciences Education*, 16(1), 1–13. https://doi.org/10.1187/cbe.16-08-0265.

Glenz, Tamara. (2014, April). The Importance of Learning Students' Names. *Journal of Best Teaching Practices*, 21–22.

Handy, Simon. (2008). Learning Student Names. *The Language Teacher*, 32(8), 27–28.

Lang, James M. (2020). *Distracted: Why Students Can't Focus and What You Can Do About It*. Basic Books, New York NY.

Middendorf, Joan. (2002). Learning Student Names. *National Teaching and Learning Forum*, 22.

O'Brien, Molly Townes, Leiman, Tania, and Duffy, James. (2014). The Power of Naming: The Multifaceted Value of Learning Students' Names. *QUT Law Review*, 14(1), 114–128.

Syverud, Kent D. (1993). Taking Students Seriously: A Guide for New Law Teachers. *Law Quadrangle*, 36(4), 23–33.

Chapter 9

Using Engagement Activities to Spark Greater Openness to Learning

Marlene Call

My goal is to create engaged learning and an enjoyable classroom. In the nursing field, when decisions impact the life of each patient, lightening the mood can spark enthusiasm. Students who feel connected, confident, and happy in class are often able to absorb more information, even if they don't care for the content being presented.

CLASS OPENERS

Students are often distracted and stressed as they enter the classroom space; to counter this I often use positive inquiry and self-care activities. We spend a few minutes of each class sharing what we're looking forward to, good news, something exciting, or something positive to set the tone. Then we vote on a class activity to bring us into our learning space which provides a way to let go of outside distractions that we cannot solve while we are in class. These activities range from meditation, Tai Chi, drumming, singing and dancing, to spending quiet time reflecting with calming nature sounds.

Along with the emotional benefit of positive inquiry, it also allows us to begin creating a sense of familiarity and community, which are essential for student success. Self-care activities set the tone that our own mental health/ well-being are essential and that they are seen as a whole person in my class-room. I have had students come long after graduation to let me know that the pre-class self-care activities helped them survive their first few months as a nurse and establish a healthier work/life balance. While not everyone loves every activity, I tell them they never know when they may have a patient who may benefit from something they've tried in the past.

Semester Engagement

Preparing students for their future career roles can often be challenging, especially if we want to engage with current events in real time. The GRASPS format creates a semester long role-playing activity each week. We begin the semester with a DQI (dilemma, question, issue) approach in the community and public health nursing course for undergraduate nursing students. Our question is: What would the top public health issues be if there were a new national government created for and occupied by a public health nurse? We use the course content and discuss current events to identify interventions towards our ultimate goal of healthcare for all.

Public health is underfunded and in working with the public we have to be able to understand and explain things in layman's terms; thus each week we break down our topics and vote to keep only the most essential (top 2–3) topics. Since presentations are often anxiety producing, we draw topics at random, and they present their running platform topics based on the highest ranked topics. We have a celebration/presentation day where we have campaign posters for the teams, and each team has 10–15 minutes to convince the rest why we should vote for their specific topics. Students have found the discussion of current events to be eye opening, with many learning for the first time about hardships and challenges that their patients face.

Chapter 10

First Day Activity Prior to Orientation and Disbursement of Syllabus

Clarence Riley

On the first day of most of my undergraduate health related courses, particularly my Human Sexuality course (appropriateness to be determined by the professor for each individual course), instead of handing out the syllabus, walk in and ask a student in the first row if they would be willing to jot down some notes for you. Tell them they simply need to number the ideas as we discuss them. Once they agree, then ask the class what they would like to learn in the course this semester (repeating the name of the course for clarity).

It usually does not take long for the first person to say something, and then the ball gets rolling. Periodically check with your student who is writing these ideas down, to see if they are able to keep up and to make them feel appreciated and respected for their contribution to this process.

As you get to a point where the ideas either begin to overlap or are a little vague, you step in to help clarify, showing your concern that you are seeking to give them exactly what they are looking for. If the session slows down or you have not covered all the topics you normally would, use one of the previously suggested topics as a jumping off point to suggest the possibility of another topic; for example, if the last topic suggested was birth control methods, ask would you also like to discuss their effectiveness. The answer will always be yes. Try not to get into a discussion of the topic itself at this point because you are simply wanting to whet their appetite.

Essentially you are engaging the class in a brainstorming technique on the first day of the class, that stimulates thought and gives them the opportunity to take ownership for the course. Likely, when all is said and done on the first day, the students will be happy to have had input into what they are going to learn in the course and you will have 95% of the topics listed that you would have covered anyway. The psychological importance of this cannot be over-stressed because professors need to create in the student's mind, the idea that their professors really care about their wishes and needs. What better way than to allow them the feeling that they are having a course customized to their needs and wishes.

Along those same lines, it is imperative to reveal something about your personal life to the students. Having a person trust you with their problems is one of the greatest compliments one can pay to another. This idea should be used by professors to let their students know they care about them enough to reveal things in their personal lives to them because of the relationship they seek to have with their students.

We need to show them that we too trust them. It does not have to be a big thing, but something that gives them the feeling that they are entrusted by you (e.g., my struggles losing weight). It really pays off in the end.

Chapter 11

How Small Teaching
Creates a Big Impact!

Sutandra Sarkar

After learning about the OneHE course on *Small Teaching: Learning Through Connecting* offered by Flower Darby and Dr. James Lang, I realized that Small Teaching is an excellent supplement to the teaching methodology I already practice in the classroom.

At Georgia State University, we teach the precalculus MATH 1113 course in a coordinated format using the Modified Emporium Model. This is a prerequisite course for many non-math major courses recommended for biology, chemistry, neuroscience, and psychology majors and is currently taught in the MILE (Mathematics Interactive Learning Environment) lab environment. Students are required to attend a 50-minute once-a-week F2F or synchronous session and twice-a-week 75-minute MILE lab sessions.

Students get the opportunity to learn the content in a student-centered learning environment with readily available free tutoring resources from the GLAs (Graduate Lab Assistants) and undergraduate SAs (Student Assistants), and faculty. Many students lack appreciation for learning these prerequisite materials as they do not see direct connections with their major programs. With only once a week in-class session, the instructor feels compelled to cover the entire course in fourteen sessions over a 14-week period. The weekly tasks involve coverage of 2–3 sections per lesson.

At the beginning, like any other instructor, I would tend to cover the materials as much as I could in that 50-minute session, using examples to relate the real-world applications. Students were then required to work on weekly assignments during their lab sessions. It was expected that regularly devoted time for the program and active work in the weekly assignments with guided practice and immediate direct assistance from the tutors would help the students learn and grasp the concepts better, and help them prepare for the next topics.

I quickly realized that solely delivering content would not keep students motivated. Therefore, I started incorporating strategies to connect concepts of interdisciplinary and upper-level courses, namely, the relevance of pre-calculus concepts in the areas of chemistry, calculus, etc. For example, I demonstrate the connections of difference quotient, composite functions, logarithmic and exponential functions, vectors, etc., at the current level and how they connect to courses like calculus and physics. Then the magic happens in the classroom!

I also deliver a few questions as an engaging activity in almost every class that allows me to collect student responses and share results with students anonymously in real-time, sparking discussion right then and there.

I have been practicing this style of teaching in my classes for the past several years, before learning about "Small Teaching." I am happy to see that the teaching practices I have developed organically align with the pedagogy. I truly see the value and the connections that happen, which I believe is the best thing that happens in my class and motivates students to come back looking forward to something new.

The OneHE course on Small Teaching has shown me new strategies to help make a difference. One important takeaway I found from this course is that a short break from the monotonous learning environment works like a charm. Therefore, I built a large database of precalculus-based conceptual questions in Learning Catalytics, which I used in class to provide an opportunity for the students to stay engaged and learn from their mistakes. This small change showed immediate improvement. To make it more meaningful, I made it a low-stakes activity as participation points which is easily achievable but has a positive impact.

My future goal is to assess learning outcomes in relation to this assignment for research purposes. Survey reports and student feedback in the evaluation indicated overall satisfaction of students' experience in the classroom environment. A small group of students did not get that boost due to inactive participation. An example of a survey response is shown in figure 11.1.

I have participated in many workshops and several conferences to learn about various tools and how these are implemented. I became aware of the free resources and utilized them in my delivery model. I feel confident that future students and I will benefit from the ideas that I picked up as a result of my participation in this Small Teaching course.

Overall, I think that my students, my fellow colleagues in my faculty community, and I will benefit from the ideas that I picked up because of my course redesign. I have found that sharing some of the strategies I have employed in my course, like Learning Catalytics, Desmos, Nearpod, etc., that

**Solve triangle ABC if a = 9.47 ft, b = 15.9 ft, and ⬚c = 21.1 ft.. Which angle   ⋮
should you solve first for this specific triangle?**

by Sutandra Sarkar · 1 month ago

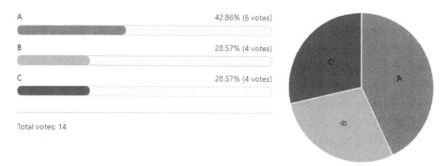

Figure 11.1.   Sample survey response from course survey. *Source: Author.*

bring everyone in one playing field is very helpful. Sharing the cumulative
responses triggers the discussion and empowers the understanding. This also
helps students to develop skills to avoid common mistakes. Some of my colleagues were inspired, and are planning to try out this sort of small teaching
strategies in their classes.

Chapter 12

An Evolution of
Engaging Students

Learning Assistants in the Classroom

Aubrey L. Dyer

For many students, especially underrepresented minorities and those without strong math backgrounds, their first chemistry course can be intimidating and a barrier to continuation in their STEM college courses. While many faculty and universities provide a variety of student success resources (office hours, tutors, supplemental instructors, etc.), many students do not take advantage of the available resources. Often, it is those most in need of that help that never do.

LEARNING ASSISTANTS

It is with the goal of reaching those at-risk students in mind that Clayton State began implementing a Learning Assistant (LA) program. The program initially begins in the biology department, and in the Spring of 2020, expanded to both math and chemistry. In the chemistry LA program, we utilized LAs in selected sections of the first semester general chemistry course geared towards STEM majors (CHEM 1211).

Learning Assistants are student peers who are embedded in the course with the goal of facilitating active learning in the classroom. The use of LAs allows the course to become student-focused, using feedback from the LAs, to adjust the course and content delivery. During the Spring 2020 semester, as was experienced worldwide, the course delivery pivoted to online and delivery modes varied in subsequent semesters in response to students needs and the limitations brought on by the pandemic.

FIRST ITERATION MODEL

Starting with the Spring of 2020, one section of a first semester Principles of Chemistry course was delivered with the majority of course time spent as a face-to-face lecture with worked example problems interspersed throughout. The students were then split into two separate, required, recitation sessions. The sessions met once a week for one hour and were focused on problem-solving activities with students working in groups of four to five. Group collaboration and problem-solving activities were facilitated by the faculty member and an LA circulating around the room.

PANDEMIC MODIFICATIONS

As courses shifted entirely online due to the pandemic quarantine requirements, so did this course. The lecture content was delivered asynchronously via video lectures and the recitation sessions were delivered via Zoom break-out rooms with students completing online activities in their established groups. The faculty member and LAs circulate amongst the break-out rooms, facilitating the groups in their problem-solving assignments.

At the conclusion of one of the most difficult semesters for students and faculty alike, the outcomes of the students in this LA-facilitated course section were markedly improved over those who were in a course section that did not have LAs. The pass rate (percentage of those students who earned an A, B, or C grade) in the sections that had an LA was an average of 98% compared to a section that did not, with a pass rate of 56%.

SUBSEQUENT ITERATIONS

Over the next several semesters, the utilization of LAs varied from facilitating group discussion boards and feedback on missed exam questions in a fully online asynchronous section (Summer 2020), to interacting with students during clicker question assignments in hybrid sections and a "coffee break" midterm feedback and success skills advice session (Fall 2020). As courses became fully in person starting in the spring of 2021, the LAs were utilized in facilitating group (as physical distancing allowed) and individual problem-solving activities.

STUDENT COMMENTS REGARDING
LAS IN THE CLASSROOM

*"The learning assistants are extremely helpful and encourage partici-
pation in class whether the students are right or wrong."*

"They make you feel encouraged . . . "

*"I enjoy the fact that I can go to the LAs for anything related to the
course and they understand the questions I ask, while being eager to
guide me in the right direction towards understanding the information."*

*"I feel more comfortable talking to them because at the end of the day
they are students too so we share something in common"*

The student success rates remained relatively high with an average pass
rate of 76.5% in LA-utilized sections compared to 73.0% in non-LA-utilized
sections. Another measure of student success is retention. A comparison of
1-year retention rates showed that, on average, 75% of students in the sections of CHEM 1211 that contained LAs returned the following year, while
67% returned in non-LA sections.

As the LA program in chemistry continues past it's second year, we have
utilized LAs in 9 separate sections of CHEM 1211 with two different faculty
members and are beginning to expand to the second semester and laboratory
courses. Faculty who have utilized LAs in their course have noted increased
engagement of the students, a sense of collaboration with the learning assistants themselves, and a building of a learning community with the students
reaching out to the LAs for advice beyond the course content. As noted by the
selection of comments from students in the course, a sense of belonging and
support is built, in addition to tangible success markers in improved percentage of ABC grades and retention.

REFERENCES

Otero, Valerie, Pollock, Steven, and Finkelstein, Noah. "A physics department's role
in preparing physics teachers: The Colorado learning assistant model." *American
Journal of Physics, 78*(11) (November 2010): 1218–1224.

Chapter 13

Using Evidence-Based Practices in Courses about Evidence

Emily G. Weigel

In the large enrollment (~150 student), upper-level Experimental Design and Biostatistics course, I frequently encounter students who have been shaped by focusing on "safe," "simple" answers. Upon starting my course, they are welcomed to the idea of non-neutrality of data and hypotheses, and—from day one—dispel the notion that completing calculations and a single correct answer are how stats really work.

Key to tackling hard problems is understanding one's thinking process, and ideally, carefully documenting it. However, students completing work tend to focus (and rush through) on the calculations, without necessarily considering the appropriateness of certain techniques. I therefore use metacognition-based, 2-stage homeworks to shift the focus to "why" rather than just "how."

WHY TWO STAGES?

This format requires students to regularly engage with the material at spaced intervals, giving distributed practice through time, which is the most efficient way to learn.[1] This means it takes students *less time* overall to get to the same level of mastery. Additionally, requiring reflection reinforces finding and fixing trouble-spots, so students achieve more than just doing problems alone.[2]

HOW DOES IT WORK?

In Stage 1, we post ~5 homework problems on an extended long scenario from a real-world experiment. Students are then to solve AND rate their own understanding (1–5, with 5 being mastery) for each problems. Grades for Stage 1 are then determined by (1) giving answers and showing work, even if incorrect, and (2) rating of one's understanding, regardless of whether a rating is high or low.

In Stage 2, students then review their Stage 1 answers relative to an answer key. For each problem, they (1) (when wrong) state specifically what they did not understand AND correct their mistakes OR (when right) explain the answer in a new, different way from the key, and (2) re-rate their understanding (which can change or stay the same, BUT serves as an indication of where to review/get help). A final homework score is simply the presence/absence of the above elements and the summed score from the stages.

HOW DO STUDENTS BENEFIT?

Students focus more on attempting and reasoning through problems, and quite a few students improve across the term. Students whose work is also absent (or that shows serious, uncorrected deficiencies) are also flagged early as potentially needing intervention.

HOW DO INSTRUCTORS BENEFIT?

With students more focused on learning, their questions are more pointed, as they are better able to articulate their struggles. Questions go from "Can you go back?" to "I see why [X], but are you doing [Y] specifically because of [Z]? I want to understand the logic." Additionally, as students are "in charge" of grading the details of their work, reviewing the keys and checking one's work is a bit more reflective than just reviewing the instructor's comments, which can sometimes be ignored. In large classes, this also decreases the grading time markedly without sacrificing feedback and revision, while also giving a record of student growth of which we and they could be proud!

NOTES

1. Rohrer & Pashler, 2007.
2. See Brockbank and McGill (2007) for a nice review.

REFERENCES

Brockbank, A., & McGill, I. *Facilitating reflective learning in higher education.* United Kingdom: McGraw-Hill Education, 2007.

Rohrer, D., & Pashler, H. Increasing retention without increasing study time. *Current Directions in Psychological Science, 16*(4), (2007): 183–186.

Chapter 14

The Legal World Is Wider Than Students Think

Monica Carol Miller

The students who signed up for the first legal writing course at MGA represented a range of majors and experiences, from a criminal justice major whose day job was working for a judge, to an aviation student who was taking the class to see if pre-law was even right for him. The students' range of interests and experiences was particularly challenging in this fully online, asynchronous class. Most of the students wanted to go to law school and be a lawyer, and they expected this class to prepare them for law school. For many students, however, their idea of being a lawyer came from television shows such as *Law and Order* and was generally limited to the field of litigation.

We used a legal writing textbook and *Westlaw,* the online legal database, as the primary resources in the class. However, I also wanted to provide more of an introduction to the law, especially for those who were completely new to the field. Given my own editing background in the legal field, which included editing the capital case handbook for the state of Tennessee, I wanted my students to learn about the myriad careers that draw upon legal writing. There's so much more to the law than courtroom drama.

Students learned the various options in the field of legal writing, along with genres of writing. Each week, a posted video interview with someone whose work includes legal writing became the subject of discussion. These interviews included the university's legal counsel, a partner in a law firm, a trainer for *LexisNexis,* and two attorneys from the Tennessee State Public Defender's Office. Each interview took approximately twenty minutes, and in each interview, I asked the following questions:

- Tell us about your background and current position?

- What role do writing and research play in your work?
- What sorts of writing and research skills do you think are important, both for a legal career and in general?
- What advice do you have for undergraduate students who are interested in a legal career?
- What else would you like the students to know?

For each interview, there was a discussion board assignment about the interview. Students identified repeated themes in the interviews, including the importance of internship opportunities, clear writing, and strong research skills. One of the interview subjects had been a stay-at-home parent for a decade after law school and talked about keeping her skills up while taking care of her children. As many of the students were parents themselves, this interview was of particular importance to them; I know that at least a couple of students have since reached out to her, per her invitation, with more specific questions about time management and parenting.

A frequent topic raised by students in the discussion boards was the search for internships in the legal field; the importance of internships was noted in nearly every interview. In response to their concerns, I contacted our Center for Career and Leadership Development (CCLD) Office, who not only provided resources about how to find internships, but also recorded a video themselves for my class, in which they talked about the ways that their office can help students find and apply for internships. I heard from several students about this information, as they not only used the links provided to search for themselves but also made appointments to meet with the CCLD.

It can be especially challenging to create connections with students in asynchronous, online classes. Having these regular video interviews with both the instructor and legal professionals helped make the class feel less impersonal and more like an authentic classroom experience. In the course evaluations, one student expressed appreciation for "growth and new perspective I've gained for the legal field." Another student commented that, "This class gave us a great deal of information and experience in legal study in just a very short time."

Given the challenges of a short class session as well as an asynchronous, online format, the video interviews played a significant role in informing and welcoming students to legal writing. The consistently positive student responses about these videos have since encouraged me to look for ways I can include similar interviews in other online courses.

Chapter 15

Service-Learning for Social Justice in General Education Courses

Stefanie Sevcik

The COVID-19 pandemic alongside the racial justice protests in summer 2020 caused me to radically rethink my relationship with my discipline, my profession, and my students. My expectations for "engagement" suddenly felt very different than they had previously, so I knew that my students would feel differently about their coursework. I also assumed that teaching online would make engagement more challenging, so I leaned into the opportunity of creating a virtual service-learning project. Among the High-impact Practices (HiPs), Community-based Engaged Learning (or, service-learning) held the promise of transforming students beyond the traditional content of my training in comparative literature.

In my interdisciplinary general education sophomore seminar, "Sex and Resistance," I connected global perspectives on women's resistance with local social justice contexts through a Critical Service-Learning (CSL) collaboration with the GCSU Women's Center & LGBTQ+ Programs. When the need for increased virtual programming arose, my students planned and hosted virtual advocacy events for the campus community.

For the first two years of the collaboration, from Fall 2020 through Spring 2022, I have taught six regular sections of the course and one Honors' section with a total of 165 student participants planning and hosting twenty-four virtual and in-person programs for the GCSU community.

CRITICAL SERVICE-LEARNING FOR SOCIAL JUSTICE

Through the lens of Critical Service-Learning (CSL) I was able to raise the stakes of my syllabus. It is not always evident how courses in world literature and media can be useful in our daily lives. By asking students to apply their insights about global feminisms to their local community, the content resonates more deeply and they gain practical experience advocating for marginalized perspectives. Beyond the typical constraints and fraught town-gown relationships that can arise through a traditional service-learning project, CSL tackles structural inequalities in a more self-reflective manner oriented toward social justice outcomes.

By creating CSL experiences "educators can create spaces where students can engage in social action to improve conditions for their communities" (Coffey and Arnold 2022). Teaching at a Predominantly White Institution (PWI), it is important for me and my students to keep diversity, equity, and inclusion in the forefront of our work together. Many of my students do not possess an adequate vocabulary for discussing matters of diversity, equity, inclusion, and social justice. In my course, we develop a vocabulary and a practice of social justice together.

ON-CAMPUS ENTITIES MAKE GREAT COMMUNITY PARTNERS

In our last QEP at GCSU, we identified four characteristics for transformative service-learning: integrating theory and practice, direct experience with the community, developing a mutually beneficial partnership, and student reflection (GC Journeys). Even without a pandemic, finding a community partner can be the most challenging element of a service-learning collaboration. I found a community partner on campus that aligned with my course outcomes and my social justice orientation: the GCSU Women's Center & LGBTQ+ Programs.

The project we co-created empowers groups of students to organize and host campus-wide virtual events around topics identified by the Women's Center as needing advocacy and attention at GCSU including power-based interpersonal violence, sexual assault, intersectionality, and LGBTQ+ rights. Each group of students researches their topic, creates a website, advertises, and organizes an event such as a panel discussion of experts as they become advocates for their issue.

VIRTUAL SERVICE-LEARNING WORKS!

Our virtual events consistently draw 15–65 participants over Zoom. The impact resonates outward from the event as they are recorded and uploaded to the GCSU Women's Center YouTube channel. Popular events, such as a panel on intersectionality, have received over ninety additional views. Since this began as a pandemic project, it has been relatively simple to bring the events from the virtual world to physical spaces. In over ten informal and formal reflections, students identify the experience as highly transformative and they are appreciative that I ask them to step outside of their comfort zone as they gain a vocabulary and toolbox as agents of social change.

Students typically describe the course as challenging, but rewarding. One participant described the experience of attending an event as transformative in terms of transferable skills: "Your event taught me to be confident in any leadership position I have in the future." One student who organized an event drew connections between local and global social justice work: "People everywhere, specifically women, are affected by laws and cultural norms all over the world. Race and gender are definitely two big topics that we need to talk about globally."

More work needs to be done to formally assess the outcomes for participants and students, but it is clear that this kind of high-impact work resonates beyond the walls of the classroom and creates more highly engaged global citizens.

REFERENCES

Coffey, H. and Arnold, L. *Transformative Critical Service-Learning: Theory and Practice for Engaging Community College and University Learners in Building an Activist Mindset.* Myers Education Press, 2022.

GC Journeys. Community-based Engaged Learning. Georgia College & State University. https://www.gcsu.edu/academics/community-based-engaged-learning

GC Women's Center. *Playlists* [YouTube Channel]. YouTube. Retrieved August 10, 2022, from https://www.youtube.com/user/GCWomensCenter/playlists

Chapter 16

Virtual Exchange Integration in Precalculus Course

Enhancing Collaboration and Learning

Sutandra Sarkar

As the recent pandemic has shown, drastic changes can occur in very little time, and flexible modes of instruction like online learning have become more crucial than ever before. However, students without a solid foundation in the subject matter or strong academic traits are less likely to participate in fully online courses than courses involving direct contact with faculty and other students. Even if these students persist with their earnest effort, their outcomes often do not live up to the expectations of the courses.

Research indicates that thoughtfully delivered distance learning is positively related to student engagement and academic achievements (Walker & Koralesky, 2021). To provide students with knowledge reinforcement and context relevance, I decided to deliver engaging instruction in a unique way, and that is through the Virtual Exchange (VE) program.

For the first time, I ventured into the VE initiative in my Precalculus program in Fall 2021. Over a 4-week period, I collaborated with a foreign institution of Nigeria. Even though some students initially posed resistance and perceived this effort to be an additional workload, I took steps to build the confidence of students at all levels. As a result, students found it was worth their time and effort, resulting in 100% student participation.

The key contributing factor was getting everyone involved through an "Icebreaker" introduction in a common space. Orientation is very important to introduce the tools and to demonstrate the project expectations for grading purposes.

What did you learn from this program?

46 responses

this experience made me aware of others at my school, as well as Ududuwa State University.

collaborative effort

How to take real world data and apply it to graphs and data

I learnt how to apply mathematics to real life activities very well than before and I also learnt alot about cooperate.

I connected with fellow GSU students and those from OUI. It was great seeing how similar all of us are despite living in different parts of the world.

Improving my problem-solving skills.

How to come together with people to carry certain objectives

To work effectively and it helped me to think critically in solving academic works and even real life problems if life.

Figure 16.1.   Sample student responses from course survey. *Provided by author.*

Ultimately, students really benefited from this inaugural effort. Figure 16.1 is a sample of student responses.

Given these promising results, I continued the VE program through this semester. The enrichment through this VE project delivery truly makes my course a signature experience.

As shown in Figure 16.2, 50% of respondents indicated collaboration as the top skill they learned through this course project. Integrating a component like VE project proves the effectiveness of High-Impact Practices (HIP) course content, aligning with the learning objective of solving a variety of mathematical modeling problems.

The VE project requires meticulous course design to tackle potential trips and falls, which will not be possible without grant support. Setting up the project is an enormous task by itself due to time zone differences, the pacing of the semester, and the availability of the partner faculty. Other challenges include delivering the project, bringing together all participants from across the globe, and holding orientation sessions. Navigating the language barrier may not be obvious.

In addition, it is essential to demonstrate the efficacy of the VE project to my peers and the wider research community. Through analysis of emerging data, future iterations of this course can continue to improve. I intend to expand the VE-based activity as a curriculum in introductory mathematics

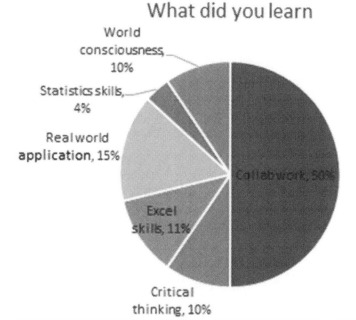

Acknowledgement: Felipe Ignacio Benitez Ulloa

Figure 16.2. Sample student responses in pie chart form. *Source: Pie chart created by grad student researcher. Provided by author.*

courses in the future and to offer workshops for colleagues to help them consider this VE project and experience the benefits themselves.

REFERENCE

Walker, K. A., & Koralesky, K. E. Student and instructor perceptions of engagement after the rapid online transition of teaching due to Covid-19. (2021). https://doi.org/10.1002/nse2.20038

Chapter 17

Writing in Mathematics (WIM)

Belinda P. Edwards

THE COURSE

To improve the proof abilities of high school students, the best place for mathematics educators and mathematicians to look is toward a proof-oriented college course for mathematics majors and pre-service mathematics teachers. A major objective of the *Introduction to Mathematics Systems* course is to teach undergraduate students how to read, write, and understand mathematics proofs.

THE CHALLENGE

Mathematics proof is a difficult concept for many students, and some are unable to construct proofs beyond simple informal proofs.[1] Research shows that many students lack the confidence in mathematics courses to transfer prior mathematics skills within advanced level mathematics coursework with proofs.[2]

WRITING IN MATHEMATICS (WIM)

WIM creates an inclusive classroom environment where students feel supported and free to learn, explore new ideas, and share their understanding in small and whole-group settings. Further, WIM provides an opportunity for students to become experts/novice-experts by developing substantial knowledge over time then accessing and sharing that knowledge with others.[3]

TYPES OF WRITING

Expository

Students write about the mathematical work of a mathematician including a detail explanation and justification.

Historical

Students show independence and critical thought by writing a history of a mathematics topic covered in class and provide an argument or critique of a finding or statement in the primary source using a secondary source.

Conjecture

Conjectural writing supports students' reasoning and proof. Students establish the validity of a statement and why it is true by writing a step-by-step logical argument verifying the truth of a conjecture or a mathematical proposition.

Computational

Computational and analytic writing represents students' mathematics knowledge interpretations and critical thinking. Students use Wolfram's Mathematica to facilitate computations or graphing while inserting text and annotations to communicate their understanding and justify their computations.

THE WRITING ASSIGNMENT (TWA)

During the semester, students learn proof techniques and mathematics content related to theorems, apply a variety of proof techniques, share their proofs with peers during small and whole-group discussions, and present alternative proofs when required. The purpose of TWA is to enable students to engage their mathematical reasoning, problem-solving, and proof skills through practice applying notation, language, and proof methods within a chosen topic, then share their understanding during a poster session.

Student Benefits

WIM supports students to communicate their mathematics understanding, make connections among mathematical ideas, and develop a deeper understanding of mathematics. Students begin thinking like mathematicians and become conversant with the language of mathematics. They begin to view themselves as individuals who belong to the community of mathematics learners and doers.[4]

Instructor Benefits

WIM can help instructors understand students' conceptual misconceptions and procedural errors, provide detailed feedback to improve student understanding, and build confidence to support mathematics learning for all students.

NOTES

1. Moore, 1994; Senk, 1985; Weber, 2001.
2. Basson, 2002; Bransford et al., 2018; Britton et al., 2005.
3. Bransford et al., 2018.
4. Thompson 2010; Boaler, 2008.

REFERENCES

Basson, I. (2002). Physics and mathematics as interrelated fields of thought development using acceleration as an example. *International Journal of Mathematical Education in Science & Technology, 33*(5), 679–690. doi:10.1080/00207390210146023

Boaler, J. (2008). Creating mathematical futures through an equitable teaching approach: The case of Railside school. *Teachers College Record, 110*(3), 606–645.

Bransford, J. D., Brown, A. L., & Cocking, R. R. (Eds.). (2018). How experts differ from novices. In *How people learn: Brain, mind, experience, and school*. National Academy Press.

Britton, S., New, P. B., Sharma, M. D., & Yardley, D. (2005). A case study of the transfer of mathematics skills by university students. *International Journal of Mathematics Education in Science and Technology, 36*(1), 1–13.

Moore, R. C. (1994). Making the transition to formal proof. *Educational Studies in Mathematics, 27*, 249–266.

Senk, S. L. (1985). How well do students write geometry proofs? *Mathematics Teacher, 78*, 448–456.

Thompson, L. S. (2010). Writing to communicate mathematically in the elementary school classroom. *Ohio Journal of School Mathematics, 61*, 36–44.

Weber, K. (2001). Student difficulty in constructing proofs: The need for strategic knowledge. *Educational Studies in Mathematics, 48*(1), 101–119.

Chapter 18

Google Docs

A Tool for Engagement and Self-Explanation

Ava Hogan-Chapman

Special Education for Elementary Educators is a first-semester course taken by juniors enrolled in the Elementary Education Educator Preparation Program in which students learn about children with exceptionalities. I employed the use of Google Docs to provide student engagement in the process of self-explanation and will share how the concept of self-explanation is beneficial for education students, particularly as demonstrating that Google Docs can show evidence of conceptual understanding.

WHY SELF-EXPLANATION?

As students learn many topics required for teaching elementary students, the vast multitude of concepts, students' new knowledge, and evolving understandings are not scorable on by exam. Therefore, the concept of "self-explanation, that helps learners modify and improve their existing perceptions or knowledge of a subject matter" appeared much more useful.[1] Student self-perception and understanding of young learners evolve continuously and therefore is a powerful strategy to stimulate a growth-mindset. "When a learner encounters instructional material that conflicts with their existing mental modes, self-explaining helps repair and revise their understanding."[2]

HOW DOES IT WORK?

In Google Docs, I create and customize a blank document for my course. An editable link is shared with students. The link remains active and accessible until the instructor restricts usage. I provide instructions for students to type responses under a specific title. Students include their private number when interacting on the document, which is shared between the student and instructor before initial use of the document. Answers are visible in real-time.

HOW DO STUDENTS BENEFIT?

Here is what students said:

- "The google document helps me see varied perspectives on the importance of each topic."
- "The google document would help me better understand topics because it gives me key words on each topic so it gives me a general idea on each topic. With this in mind, I feel like the document would've probably helped me finish my assignments quicker since I would have not taken so much time rereading chapters to understand them."
- "I think we can all say we felt more connected. This experience helped us connect because in a way it helped us share emotions, thoughts, and perspectives together. For once we got to see other's perspectives on topics in a google document 'live.' Since it was 'live,' we got to see other's Immediate thoughts which was cool. This exercise also made me feel like we were all engaged with the material. Overall, it was an experience that one way or another benefit us."

HOW DO INSTRUCTORS BENEFIT?

The instructors become practitioners of inclusive and responsive teaching as students encounter new information. Using this strategy promotes validation for students' diverse perspectives while building community. Curriculum becomes accessible to all and promotes a deeper sense of learning. Using Google Docs for self-explanation can be useful for the evaluation of students' conceptual understanding.

NOTES

1. Lang, 2018, p. 147.
2. Chiu and Chi, 2014, p. 92, as cited in Lang, 2018, p. 147.

REFERENCES

Lang, James. *Small Teaching: Everyday Lessons from the Science of Learning.* Hoboken, NJ: Jossey-Bass, 2018.

Chapter 19

Creating Cultures of Creative Critical Thinking and Self-Reflection in the College Arts Classroom

Laura McCloskey Wolfe

Creative and critical thinking, as well as using self-reflective assignments, are High-Impact and Brain-Based Practices that activate the prefrontal cortex of the brain (governing mindset, among other abilities) and promote neural connections across multiple brain regions to bring "awareness of feeling into thinking."[1] These practices are also logical extensions of Bloom's Taxonomy, which relies on progressively moving from the following levels: remember, understand, apply, analyze, evaluate, and create.[2]

In my introductory-level art history courses, I utilize these theories to encourage interdisciplinary and cross-cultural connections that help students see the holistic value of their coursework. These aspects are critical to student motivation to learn and academic perseverance: factors which are particularly important in contemporary diverse learning environments.[3]

EXPERIENTIAL LEARNING WITHIN THE ARTS CLASSROOM

In an effort to help students appreciate cultural and spiritual diversity in my Western Art from Ancient to Medieval course, I created an exercise that purposely allows them to suspend judgment regarding the artwork they see, focusing instead on the terminology that I teach them regarding formal analysis. This helps students contemplate the artistic elements present in new

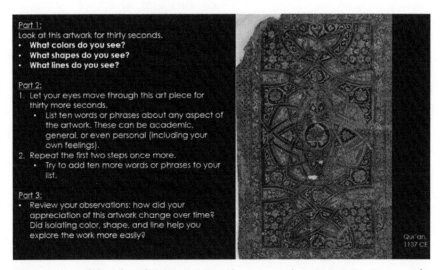

Figure 19.1. Slide of a three-part art assignment, using Q1137CE. *Source: The Metropolitan Museum of Art, public domain.*

art pieces for which they may have little to no background knowledge or expectations. First we used the slide featured in figure 19.1 for contemplative practice to analyze the components of Islamic art and design.[4]

Next, we discussed that this was an image from the religious book the Qur'an, and I provided artistic and historical context for this manuscript. Finally, I showed students three different examples of Qur'an folios, including the one already shown, and asked them to write a brief analysis of the images based on our discussions.[5] We also explored the similarities between Christian, Judaic, and Islamic book arts as a way to help students open their minds to different cultural perspectives.

The slide used in the follow-up reflective written response is shown in figure 19.2.

DATA AND IMPLICATIONS

Data collected from this exercise was qualitative, and thus subjective. After using this exercise for three years and with nearly one hundred students, unit quiz responses suggest that students were able to successfully connect this activity to more in-depth analytical short essay prompts that asked them to compare folios from multiple religious texts.

Student responses to this activity have been overwhelmingly positive, with remarks such as:

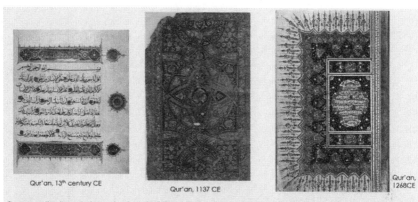

Compare the formal elements of each of these Qur'an folios: how does the treatment of line, form, color, rhythm, movement, unity, and balance differ in each piece? What elements appear to be the same or similar? How is text integrated into the design of the folio (if text is present)? These folios are from the same sacred text, but clearly different in design: what can this tell us about spirituality in Islamic book arts? Why might that be important to studying art history? Do these folios remind you of any books or other art pieces that you have seen or that we have studied in previous weeks?

Figure 19.2.   Slide using three Qur'an folios of different dates. *Source: The Metropolitan Museum of Art, public domain.*

- "This exercise helped me see the rhythm and natural beauty of the piece as my eye was led around the work."
- "After doing this activity I noticed areas that were not obvious at first, like foliage, interlacing knots, filigree swirls, and even empty spaces."
- "This helped me understand the Islamic religion. I think balance and unity are the main principles that stand out more than the others. To have balance, you can't have too much negativity, and unity means coming together as one; the differences don't matter. I believe that the creators use these specific artistic principles to show that the Quran values these principles and provides a basic understanding of what Islam is about."
- "The more I looked at the first example, the more I felt a sense of peace and reassurance, which made sense since I learned that it was from a religious book."

Presenting content in a manner that activates a student's natural curiosity and removes judgment can potentially assist students in adopting a growth mindset. Students move from passively consuming course content to feeling as if their perspectives and the views of their classmates matter. Repeatedly utilizing these sorts of techniques within the classroom creates critical thinking and self-reflection routines that students can employ beyond the college setting. Moreover, this type of open-ended reflective exercise could easily be adapted into any art or art history classroom that utilizes the foundational principles of design and/or cross-cultural content.

CONCLUSION

From brain-based theoretical perspectives, self-reflective learning strategies have been shown to decrease stress levels and increase cognitive neuroplasticity in the frontal lobe which can be helpful in reducing a student's negativity bias in regards to course content while increasing confidence regarding their perceived ability to succeed in a course despite challenges or personal setbacks.[6] Embedding these exercises with critical thinking prompts has the potential to transform liberal arts courses through deep learning experiences for students that can translate into better grades as well as meaningful connections to future employment.[7] Further, these are High-Impact Practices that can be utilized to increase the positive reception of inclusive pedagogies.

NOTES

1. Ira Rabois, *Compassionate Critical Thinking: How Mindfulness, Creativity, Empathy, and Socratic Questioning Can Transform Teaching*, Rowman & Littlefield Publishers, 2016. *ProQuest Ebook Central*, https://ebookcentral-proquest-com.mutex.gmu.edu/lib/gmu/detail.action?docID=4729890.

2. Mary Forehand, "Bloom's Taxonomy: Original and Revised," in M. Orey (Ed.), *Emerging Perspectives on Learning, Teaching, and Technology*, CreateSpace Independent Publishing Platform, 2012.

3. Laura E. McCloskey, "Mindfulness as an Intervention for Improving Academic Success Among Students with Executive Functioning Disorders," *Procedia, Social and Behavioral Sciences* 174 (2015): 221–226.

4. The prompts used in this slide are adapted from commonly used phrases in art-based guided meditation and in museum practices such as those found at the Philadelphia Museum of Art: https://www.philamuseum.org/doc_downloads/education/lessonPlans/Digging-Deep%20Elements%20of%20Art.pdf; The Museum of Fine Arts, Houston: https://www.mfah.org/learn/practice-looking-art; and The Chazen Museum of Art: https://chazen.wisc.edu/wp-content/uploads/2020/12/Activism-through-Art_Learning-Activities.pdf.

5. This part of the activity was inspired by Eve Eisenstadt's formal analysis exercise available at https://artsoftheislamicworld.qc.cuny.edu/Lesson%20Plans/Visual%20Analysis.pdf.

6. See Sara W. Lazar, Catherine E. Kerr, Rachel H. Wasserman, Jeremy R. Gray, Douglas N. Greve, Michael T. Treadway, and Metta McGarvey, "Meditation Experience Is Associated with Increased Cortical Thickness." *Neuroreport* 16, no. 17 (2005): 1893–1897. This can be particularly true when students encounter writing intensive courses for the first time, or courses outside of their major that are historically or anecdotally viewed as difficult.

7. Ernest T Pascarella, et al., "How the Instructional and Learning Environments of Liberal Arts Colleges Enhance Cognitive Development," *Higher Education* 66, no. 5 (2013): 569–583.

Chapter 20

Understanding Friction

Using a Faculty Learning Community to Promote Student Success and Faculty Satisfaction

Robert R. Bleil

From 2002 to 2022, more than 3,600 books and articles were published on reducing barriers in higher education. Many of these works focus on large-scale choke points such as standardized admissions testing; textbook, transportation, and housing costs; and the lack of reliable broadband access in rural counties. Despite significant institutional efforts to improve success, students continue to report high levels of anxiety, stress, and disengagement.

In the 2021 National Survey of Student Engagement (NSSE), 74% of first-year female students and 56% of first-year male students reported experiencing "mental or emotional exhaustion" and more than 50% of female respondents and 40% of male respondents reported an "inability to concentrate."[1] Faculty also report that students are frequently disengaged, distracted, and unprepared for class. How do faculty engage students consistently and effectively in the face of these significant challenges, and how do chairs support faculty in these efforts?

Institutions often respond to these challenges with public initiatives, increased surveillance, and hierarchical reporting. But programmatic responses have had inconsistent success, and their recommendations often require significant investment and time before results can be evaluated. In response to these hurdles, faculty in the Department of Arts and Humanities at the College of Coastal Georgia formed a series of local, limited, and focused faculty learning communities (FLCs) that address specific challenges in real time. With their flexible structure, low start-up costs, and local governance; FLCs have proven to be an effective, nimble, and sustainable method for managing and reducing unnecessary friction. FLCs allow faculty to focus on discrete challenges and see measurable results, and they allow chairs to address common concerns efficiently.

In February 2020, eleven faculty across four disciplines formed an FLC to address the lack of student engagement with out-of-class reading. Drawing on research into brain-based learning and pedagogical design, the participants sought to understand the relationship between reading, friction, memory, and student success. Instead of revising their entire course and waiting months for results, participants in the learning community revised a single assignment to increase transparency and engagement. The goal was to reduce unproductive friction in a gateway course while generating useful energy from sustained engagement. By keeping the FLC membership small and the goals specific, faculty participants and their students were able to see the impact of course-level changes in real time.

Shortly after the learning community formed, the initial wave of COVID-19 disrupted in-person activities and the FLC became a site for both exploration and just-in-time support. The compact and local structure of the FLC enabled participants to pivot to even smaller sites of inquiry as the pandemic evolved. Instead of disbanding after the initial fifteen-week commitment, the participants elected to continue as both a community of practice and a rapid response team.

Flower Darby's *Small Teaching Online* (2019) was one of many works which helped participants to translate their classroom expertise to new sites of instruction. Since online learning is frequently asynchronous, participants focused on transparency in learning and teaching (TiLT) to further reduce unnecessary friction and promote success.

While the initial FLC focused on specific and hyper-local adjustments to individual assignments and courses, collective knowledge generated by the FLC is having a programmatic impact on the department. In addition to a deep dive into the works of Flower Darby and James Lang, several members of the department have completed the introductory Quality Matters training. By pooling our expertise, the FLC is developing a flexible course shell that faculty will be able to deploy as they revise and expand their course offerings. In this way, the FLC has scaled-up their activities to benefit the larger community by focusing on the local moments where faculty and students can achieve tangible and concrete benefits by reducing friction across gateway courses.

When I first participated in an FLC as a graduate student more than twenty years ago, the purpose of the program was to achieve programmatic consistency across dozens of sections of the same core course. However, the last two years have shown that FLCs can support both individual faculty progress and department-level realignment.

NOTE

1. Center for Postsecondary Research, Indiana University School of Education, "The Pandemic and Student Engagement: Trends, Disparities, and Opportunities," Evidence-Based Improvement in Higher Education (2021), https://nsse.indiana.edu/research/annual-results/2021/story1.html.

PART II

Pedagogies of Engagement
at the Program Level

Chapter 21

Program Innovation with Student Learning Strategies

Jeffery Galle and Jo Galle

This book has presented eight types of innovative practices, the pedagogies of engagement, that faculty can undertake *for* students or *with* students to create a deeper learning experience for them: course design, academic inquiry, mindset strategies, inclusive teaching strategies, classroom engagement strategies and pedagogy, the High-Impact Practices (HIPs), the design of student assignments and other work, and the assessment of learning.

When applied by faculty, these practices are "teaching moves," or, in terms of impact on their students, these are "learning moves." At the individual course level, the impact of these moves has been charted by multiple individual studies.[1] Employing the learning moves more broadly at the program level can also greatly impact learning.

To be successful, professional development for faculty in the pedagogies of engagement must be embedded in the core programming of centers for teaching and learning, New Faculty Orientation programs, and similar programs. Departmental evaluations should be revised to include pedagogical performance and other categories that require further professional development outside the graduate degrees faculty have already earned. These are programs where faculty professional development is specifically intended to improve student engagement.

Programs of another type, those that specifically involve students directly, also can consider exploring and integrating various of the pedagogies of engagement where a good fit is possible. What this would involve varies from program to program, but the argument advocating for it goes something like the contexts of the following examples.

A student-focused program, the Momentum Year, ventures into the complex areas of student learning with five primary tasks for students to complete (and the institution to support) for a successful first year of college—making a purposeful program choice, finishing initial English and math, completing the first thirty hours, nine of which should be in the academic focus area, and finally, creating a productive Academic Mindset. Some of the five emerge from data that shows students who reach first year milestones are more likely to continue into the second year and beyond.

The fifth element of the Momentum Year, creating a productive Academic Mindset, has sparked exploration of the academic and pedagogical dimensions of student learning, persistence, and progression. The success of Momentum Year brought about the Momentum Approach, a focus on the full undergraduate experience. The five elements of this more comprehensive model for student successful learning extended elements of choice, the Academic Mindset into multiple mindsets, maintained focus on the clear degree pathway, achieved milestones, and finally deepened Academic Focus.

The implications of Momentum Year and Approach prompt faculty and other academic leaders to identify the strategies that support the student Academic Focus and achievement of milestones. In fact, these strategies and activities are the products of a statewide effort emerging from the Momentum Approach effort. The Chancellor's Learning Scholars program tested the idea that the development of an Academic Mindset can result from the application of a set of student learning strategies as explored in hundreds of learning communities across a state's institutions.

After three years of learning communities which explored the impact of selected pedagogies upon student learning, many participants discerned the benefits of extending this program model in their own institution. It was this statewide program begun by Dr. Tristan Denley that led to the idea that acquiring pedagogical expertise and skill in these strategies that are not taught in graduate school can really support faculty in their teaching and students in their learning. The program led to many students acquiring the Academic Mindset so fundamental to learning and to the eventual earning of a degree.

Perhaps the benchmark student success program is housed at Georgia State University. Tim Renick, Executive Director of the National Institute for Student Success at Georgia State University, has pioneered programs in this area.[2] Built around data gathering, an excellent advising system, and a number of interventions, this program may offer opportunities to employ a number of the pedagogies of engagement. In such programs, mindset principles and strategies can be applied to adviser training sessions, if they have not already, with a modicum of effort. These principles added to the playbook can influence more impactful interaction with students. Inclusive teaching principles as found in lists at Georgetown, Emory, and Stanford sites can also lend support to efforts within the National Institute for Student Success.

A program funded by the Bill Gates Foundation, the Frontier Set, defines its vision for institutional transformation in this way: a diverse group of colleges, universities, and state systems working together to go further and faster as a group, generating big ideas that can ripple outward and transform the postsecondary system as a whole—this is the foundation of the Frontier Set.[3]

The 2020 Frontier Set Annual conference program booklet contains the priorities[4] for each institution. One member, Sam Houston State, has the priority to "increase the number of students enrolled in the newly redesigned (still optional) first-year seminar course" and Arizona State University, another member, sets one of its priorities to "improve the quality of undergraduate and graduate education."

Improving enrollment and quality are not inherently contradictory, as if an institution must add qualities external to academics to increase interest and thereby enrollment. Similarly, increasing quality means precisely the focus of this chapter—adding "pedagogies of engagement" to all existing undergraduate programs will add a complexity of delivery that will ensure deeper learning for more students and learning for a greater diversity of students.

If what is meant by quality is rigor with support that leads to the outcomes desired by the institution—retention through graduation, deeper learning, and greater demand for the programs—then enriching current programs with strategies that engage students to learn can support these outcomes.

A good number of institutions already possess a First Year Experience program, an Undergraduate Research program, Writing Intensive courses, internships, or a study abroad program, to mention a few of the eleven HIPs that are typically broadened into a program of many instances of the individual practice.

Advocating for the enrichment of existing HIP programs runs the risk of being redundant, but the pedagogies of engagement offer not only the HIPs but also a number of additional "teaching moves" that may be of additional benefit to existing HIP programs.

Because the AACU's Eight Key Elements is integral to doing well with the existing HIPs, we can take a look at these elements first: appropriate level of rigor, significant time commitment, quality interactions with all involved, diversity experiences, constructive feedback, opportunities for reflection of experiences, applying content, and public presentation.

The quality of a HIP program depends on the integration of multiple elements into each instance of the program for its successful implementation, for its quality. Just as a HIP that is done well depends on integrating the key elements, so do quality courses depend on very similar integration of the pedagogies of engagement—design, inquiry, mindset, inclusion, classroom engagement, transparent real-world assignments, and assessment of learning. In fact, many of the Eight Key Elements overlap in very good ways with the pedagogies of engagement. Hence, working to ensure that a particular HIP program is well done is in many ways synonymous with enriching existing courses with "teaching moves."

In addition to programs designed for students, others equip faculty with knowledge and skill to do a good job of teaching. One set of programs is those offered by teaching and learning centers. The Boyer Report 2030 issues a call for and a vision for improvement of undergraduate education at research universities. The report contains specific recommendations for senior leadership to support Centers for Teaching and Learning and to rely on them for knowledge and skill in developing campus plans for equity and excellence.[5] Similar recommendations might reasonably be offered to all in higher education, not only to the research institutions.

Programming at teaching centers is regularly recognized for its quality and for its informal approach to participation. With additional resources given to the centers and support from institutional leaders, the programming may easily reach a majority of faculty. Joined with New Faculty Academy programs, New Faculty Orientation programs, or a teaching institute created for the explicit purpose of developing expertise across the institution, the teaching center can lead and also join with other events and programs to lessen the burden of carrying out the vision for faculty pedagogical excellence.[6]

A final kind of program that can benefit from integrating the pedagogies of engagement are a number of collaborations between academic and campus life. The identification of a "divine comity" between academic affairs and student affairs that James Cook and Christopher Lewis described can lead to the best kinds of programs for students.[7]

The student affairs divisions at some institutions manage the First Year Seminar (FYS), collaborating with faculty to co-facilitate sections of the FYS which also include students trained by student affairs. In this program, students and faculty co-teach a program whose syllabus and content is a collaboration between the two sides of the campus and the product of a committee on which sit students, faculty, and student life professionals. Students who take each section have the pleasure of working both with faculty and with staff: in addition, some of them can become student members of the managing committee.

As strong as programs like these already are, they also present a fantastic opportunity to embed mindset, inclusion, knowledge of HIPs, elements of feedback, and perhaps even TiLT in the syllabus of the FYS course.

Much of what is beneficial within individual academic courses may also be considered for larger institutional programs of many kinds. As more faculty and staff develop further expertise in strategies that lead to student and institutional success, both courses and programs will reflect greater learning outcomes. These efforts are completed within the institution by its own professionals.

A tempting option that many institutions take is the expensive prospect of hiring a vendor to do the work of the faculty, teaching center, and student life professionals on course and program innovation.[8]

Hence a path forward, certainly not the only pathway, can include both of the following features:

1. Create a Toolkit of pedagogy for student learning and disseminate the Toolkit at campus events, celebrate those who helped create it, and place it on the institution's website.
2. Support an institutional learning community program, a program that focuses on integrating these elements into every course and program.

NOTES

1. The work of Carol Dweck, Mary Murphy, and scientists at Motivate Lab are three examples of professionals furthering work on mindset. Sam Museus's work on inclusive pedagogies and culturally relevant teaching is well known. Multiple experiments with each of the HIPs have been conducted and the work of AACU's Carol G. Schneider, President Emeritus of AACU, has reinforced the deep learning of the eleven HIPs when done well. Classroom activities hearken back to "active learning" work done in the late '90s by many educators and researchers. The gift of Transparency in Learning and Teaching by Mary-Ann Winkelmas has been followed by numerous studies on the efficacy of TiLT in redesigning student assignments. Also, Virginia S. Lee's influential volume on Inquiry-Guided Learning has fostered and supported a number of Inquiry efforts and in 2014 an international gathering at Oxford College organized by Oxford College's Institute for Pedagogy in the Liberal Arts, celebrated Inquiry programs across the world. Finally, such Scholarship of Teaching and Learning (SoTL) scholars as Nancy Chick, Peter Felton, among many others have both offered their own assessment of learning experiments and urged the inclusion of assessment of learning as integral to every teaching and learning context.

2. Tim Renick, Executive Director NISS, has established a data driven process for identifying students who may be heading for academic difficulty and for intervening in successive, smart ways to address specific kinds of challenges that cause students to leave the university. Data, trained advisers, and a multifaceted intervention program have resulted in a 22-point increase in graduation rates at Georgia State University over the past ten years.

3. The Frontier Set website lays out the membership, purpose, and resources of this program dedicated to campus transformation: https://www.frontierset.org/what-is-the-frontier-set/.

4. The quotes for Sam Houston State and Arizona State are taken from the 2020 program booklet *Realizing Transformation Together*, 13, 50.

5. The Boyer Report 2030, entitled *The Equity/Excellence Imperative: A 2030 Blueprint for Undergraduate Education at U.S. Research Universities*. Specific recommendations regarding teaching centers are found on pages 28 and 53. The report is found here: https://ueru.org/boyer2030.

6. The central recommendations from the Boyer Report 2030 to support the teaching center and rely on that expertise can also be achieved by integrating pedagogical elements into other programs that exist to orient and develop faculty, such as the NFO. Oxford College of Emory also hosted an institute that offered multiple tracks with recognized pedagogical scholars leading individual two-day programs over a four-day institute. This institute lasted for ten years and influenced the teaching of faculty from Oxford College, each of the schools of Emory, and a high number of faculty outside of Emory. Such an institute could provide a model for other institutions hoping to develop further programs in addition to a teaching center.

7. James H. Cook and Christopher A. Lewis, eds., *The Divine Comity* (NASPA: 2007).

8. Institutions and a CTL network supported by a strong state system office can develop the necessary innovations in a much more sustainable way, in a way that can spread across all courses and programs and involve the professionals who lead them. Purchasing a platform or hiring an outside entity to do this work is not only expensive. It also deprives the professionals within the institution the opportunity to grow and lead. Spending resources on internal professionals is in this author's view a good use of resources.

Chapter 22

An Effective Institutional Data Communication Plan

Jesse Bishop

GEORGIA HIGHLAND COLLEGE

A strong data communication plan and a committed team of individuals to make sense of those data can lead to success in supporting a variety of initiatives. In this section, I want to highlight the work of two student success projects, Gateways to Completion (G2C) and Momentum Approach (Momentum), and how those large-scale institutional projects influenced and were impacted by data and communicating those data.

Georgia Highlands College participated in the G2C project, led by The John N. Gardner Institute (JNGI). G2C was a project that used institutional and course-level data to identify gateway courses that might pose obstacles for students. Through targeted data collection and analyses, along with concomitant faculty development, the G2C project was focused on improving student outcomes by making explicit the relationships between data and development. Likewise, the USG Momentum Year (later developed into Momentum Approach) allowed institutions to collect data around specific aspects of the student experience to identify and work toward reducing barriers in a student's academic career. While G2C was focused on course transformations, Momentum was more focused on institutional transformation.

The data collected for G2C were valuable; however, the communication plan for using those data made faculty uncomfortable because of the transparency of the project. Because the results of the data collection were shared in larger meetings with the G2C "Steering Committee," some faculty felt exposed by the number of individuals seeing disaggregated data, many of whom were instructional colleagues. This new level of transparency concerned many who saw the move as punitive rather than developmental, as "a way to out bad teaching," despite that never being the intent.

This was one of the first challenges resulting in our internal communication plan. Because we did not have a clear and effective data communication plan institutionally, the apprehension surrounding this *seemingly* new practice of analyzing course-level data for trends in DFW rates made faculty unnecessarily nervous.

There were other issues that arose from the weak communication plan. The first issue was that once faculty were aware of the data and had time to analyze them, they wanted immediate changes in their classroom practices. The absence of a stronger communication strategy led many faculty to implement more than one course-level change at a time—some because they felt "called out" and others because they were genuinely excited about having data available to inform their course-level instructional decisions. Confusing the G2C language of "course transformation" with large-scale transformational changes, instead of small-scale adaptive change, led some of our faculty to take on too much and create unsustainable workloads.

About half-way through the five-year G2C project, some of the USG efforts on Complete College Georgia (CCG) began to grow into Momentum Year. Because Momentum was focused on larger-scale institutional change, as opposed to course-level changes, and because several of us had been heavily involved with G2C and understood some of the challenges in our planning for change, we had a better sense of how to communicate the change process, especially about data around faculty development.

Whereas the G2C project relied on a more distributed and open model of data sharing, we were able to centralize the data and develop a stronger plan for communicating the purpose, activities, and outcomes of the project. This led to better and more frequent communication across units about the goals, strategies, and outcomes of the project. Momentum had fewer meetings with faculty than G2C but more frequent and stronger communication because of a more focused, intentional effort at communicating locally.

While Momentum was less focused on individual classrooms, it still featured a significant focus on faculty development and the use of data, albeit on a much broader scale. Instead of focusing on individual course transformations, our team was able to identify themes within our project scope (purposeful choice, mindset, clearer pathways, etc.) that allowed us to use data around these concepts to develop a more systematic institutional approach to faculty development and change management. We were able to use a variety of existing committees to distribute information about the project and its progress, relying on centralized reporting and analyses, rather than individualized foci.

Moreover, we have since included elements of Momentum into our strategic plan and into our annual student and employee surveys to better understand the various impacts this work is having. The results of this work are shared through several meetings with personnel from all levels of the college.

Data communication is essential in any large-scale initiative. Learning from our challenges with G2C, Georgia Highlands College was able to use Momentum Approach to better communicate our efforts in a large-scale project that has had a profound impact on students. Through strong communication planning and change management, we have seen far more effective results of Momentum work that has changed students' lives and academic trajectories.

Chapter 23

Listening Without Speaking

Making the Need for Equity Real

Devon Fisher and Jessica O'Brien

THE PROBLEM

In the aftermath of the murder of George Floyd and the inequities exposed anew by the global COVID-19 pandemic, faculty at our small university renewed their commitment to tackle problems of diversity, equity, and inclusion (DEI). Lenoir-Rhyne's Center for Teaching & Learning, in collaboration with the University's Vice-President for Diversity, Equity, and Inclusion, developed a semester-long course redesign program to help faculty address structural concerns within their courses. We faced a challenge. How could we focus the course redesign program locally? How could we help faculty to think not (only) about national problems surrounding DEI, not about DEI as a conceptual problem but as *our* problem on *our* campus that adversely affects the lives of *our* students sitting in *our* classes?

THE SOLUTION

Sometimes the best answers are the most obvious. As part of our DEI Course Redesign program, we share with faculty strategies for promoting diversity and inclusion in their classrooms, one of the most important of which is creating opportunities for students to share their own stories.[1] You can imagine that if this were a comic strip, the next panel would be a lightbulb popping on in a thought bubble over our heads. We know that storytelling can be a powerful pedagogical tool[2] and we know that actively listening is essential in DEI work.[3] Our solution, as simple as it sounds, was to use the very principles

91

we were sharing with faculty—to create the opportunity for our students to tell the stories of their own experiences. Thus we invited a panel of students to join our DEI Course Redesign program on day one to tell us their answers to one overarching question: "What is it like to be a student of color at Lenoir-Rhyne University?"

IMPLEMENTATION

Our primary consideration as we invited students to tell their stories was to ensure that they felt safe while doing so. We sent to students ahead of time our main question and another eight follow-up questions. Our course redesign sessions were virtual, taking place on Zoom, and we leveraged that technology to create a space as safe as possible. Students logged in to the meeting with a pseudonym, and we invited them to leave their cameras turned off if that helped them feel more comfortable. Finally, and most importantly, the faculty and staff who were redesigning their courses were not to speak during that part of the session. No comments. No questions. Only listening. In acknowledgment of their courage in sharing, we offered students a gift card to a place of their choice.

THE RESULTS

To this point, we have had three cohorts of faculty participate in our student listening panel. One of those groups has fully completed the course redesign program; the other two are at various stages of completions. The immediate reaction of each group to the student panel was stunned silence. A common reaction from our faculty ran along the lines of "I knew this was a problem here, but . . ." But this made me painfully aware that students sitting in my class view their dorm room as the only safe space on campus. But this made me see how my use of group work in my pedagogy needs to be rethought to ensure learning for all of my students. But this made me really understand the need to help students respond to stereotype threat.

Furthermore, while only one of our cohorts has completed the full program, focus group discussions with that set of faculty suggest that the student listening session played a key role in creating in them a desire for change.

EXTENSIONS

How might this kind of real listening session extend beyond our individual course redesign program? At the very least, we recommend this kind of listening in any DEI-focused course redesign session. Beyond that, however, we recommend it for a range of sessions. Inspiring change in faculty can be hard work. Listening to students tell their stories of what it is like to experience whatever thing it is we wish to change will, we are convinced, be a prime motivator for the sorts of change that educational developers hope to bring about.

NOTES

1. Verschelden, 2017.
2. See for instance Landrum, Brakke, & McCarthy, 2019.
3. See for instance Sue, 2013.

REFERENCES

Landrum, R. E., Brakke, K., & McCarthy, M. A. (2019). The pedagogical power of storytelling. *Scholarship of Teaching and Learning in Psychology, 5*(3), 247–253. https://doi.org/10.1037/stl0000152.

Sue, D. W. (2013). Race talk: The psychology of racial dialogues. *American Psychologist. 68*(8), 663–672. https://doi.org/10.1037/a0033681.

Verschelden, C. (2017). *Bandwidth recovery*. Sterling, VA: Stylus.

Chapter 24

Creating DEI Opportunities for Faculty

Donna Troka

For the last ten years, I have worked with faculty, graduate students, post docs, and staff across campus to develop various Diversity, Equity, and Inclusion (DEI) resources at my university. My approach has been reactive, proactive, and multimodal. Below I will outline some of the programs we have put in place over time and the impact they have had thus far.

Our early work in this area was almost exclusively reactive. Faculty came to us expressing concerns from their undergraduate and graduate students and asked for our help. We responded with two approaches. First, we developed trainings or discussion sessions on topics like "microaggressions" or "unconscious bias." Shortly after the inception of the Black Lives Matter movement we added "Anti-Racist Pedagogy," "Decolonizing Your Curriculum," and "Social Justice Pedagogies."

Secondly, we developed an Inclusive Pedagogy Handbook that offers up resources on the above topics and many more. This is a living document that we add to every year in an effort to keep it current (recent examples are "teaching during politically tumultuous times" or "teaching during a pandemic"). As time went on, and we developed robust resources on the topics that faculty were requesting, we were also able to fold in more proactive resources on topics such as "How to Navigate Difficult Conversations," "Navigating Allyship," and "Gender Diversity." These were topics that emerged from national discussions and in Higher Ed as well as in general American society.

Our next mode of DEI work is Academic Learning Communities or ALCs. These are seminar-like discussions that bring together faculty, staff, graduate students, and post docs to discuss various topics. Participants do common readings, viewings (short films or documentaries), and listenings (podcasts are becoming a more common resource to utilize) and meet between four and six times a semester to discuss them.

Not all of our ALCs are DEI focused, but many are. Topics have included "Mass Incarceration in the American South," "Mentoring Diverse Students in Lab Settings," or "Data Driven DEI at the University." Each of our ALCs not only bring together a wide variety of people from different fields and positions at the university, they also encourage participants to develop some "output" or "deliverable" that informs the rest of the campus community on the topic. In the past, DEI focused ALCs have developed white papers, websites, or faculty resource toolkits.

Our last modality of DEI work is a brand-new pilot that will take place over the 2022–2023 academic year. This will be a DEI Teaching Fellowship modeled off our already existing Center for Faculty Development and Excellence (CFDE) Teaching Fellows program. The goal of this program is to support and develop faculty who want to build competencies in DEI and apply those competencies in the classroom, lab, and/or clinical settings. DEI Teaching Fellows will do research, engage with a curriculum that will give them an understanding of foundational DEI concepts, and then develop a training or discussion session on a DEI-related topic. It is our hope that these DEI Teaching Fellows can then join the cohort of faculty and staff that already do DEI work on campus.

While these programs are robust in that they engage campus community members who are passionate and dedicated to DEI work, they only scratch the surface of the needs of our campus. Slowly, the university is developing an infrastructure for DEI work. Most, if not all, of our schools have some sort of DEI initiative led by faculty or staff members. As of 2019, we have a Chief Diversity Officer that serves the whole enterprise (both academic and health-care). And curriculum and structures are changing to reflect the demographic changes on our campus and in the world. For example, Emory College has developed a Race and Ethnicity requirement for undergraduates, class rosters can include a student's pronoun (if they opt in), and our learning management system Canvas includes the name pronunciation tool Name Coach. My hope is that all the DEI work on campus can become better connected and funded.

In the past year (AY 2021–2022), the CFDE had just over 2,000 (faculty, graduate student, post-doc, staff) contacts in DEI or Inclusive Pedagogy. A contact is a unique engagement with a person on campus, but some people may attend multiple programs and therefore will count for multiple contacts. Participants have called our sessions "excellent," "the best they have ever attended," and have said a session was "fantastic . . . I don't know if it exceeded my expectation as everything from CFDE is so great. But assume excellence!!" Others said they "valued the conversational, collaborative mode." Finally, after a recent session, the dean (who attended the session) said the DEI work in the CFDE is "single-handedly shaping the culture of [her] school."

Chapter 25

Establishment of Centers to Support Faculty and Students

Tyler Yu

The School of Business (SBA) at Georgia Gwinnett College (GGC) has a Bachelor of Business Administration (BBA) degree and has recently added a Bachelor of Science in Management Information Systems (BS-MIS). SBA is accredited by AACSB and has a mission focused on student engagement and success. Its faculty, currently at about sixty full-time and about fifteen part-time, are encouraged to do professional development for their teaching excellence and stay relevant and current in their research. As an AACSB-accredited school, we are also expected to work with the business community to make societal impact.

We use a "Center" approach to meet these expectations. Initiated by the faculty, SBA formed four centers: the Business, Economic, and Applied Research (BEAR) Center, the Center for International Business and Exchange (CIBE), the Center for Emerging Business and Entrepreneurship (CEBE), and the Leadership and Management Development Institute (LMDI). Each center has a three-prong synergy for student engagement and success, faculty research, and community outreach and service.

Embedded in the centers' missions are four high-impact practices (HIPs) commonly fostered in academia. That is, CIBE is in charge of studies abroad, CEBE facilitates internships, BEAR helps students with undergraduate research, and LMDI organizes service-learning projects. Each center also collaborates with internal and external stakeholders to make societal impact. Since research/publication is required, faculty also use the centers as their venues to conduct research directly related to the centers' missions.

BENEFITS OF THE CENTERS

Although these centers were first suggested to the Dean of SBA by faculty, I quickly saw that creating these centers was a way to promote faculty leadership, as well as a way to encourage excellence in teaching, research, and service. Through establishing directorships for the faculty who lead these centers, the directors work with their fellow faculty, with students, and with members of the business community. In exchange, the directors receive public recognition for their services. The Dean's Office publicly acknowledges their work on the GGC website, in the Dean's Newsletter (which comes out at least twice a year), and at the Dean's regular faculty meetings.

The directors do not receive a stipend or a course release. Of all of these methods of rewarding the directors, the one that the directors seem to appreciate the most is the public praise and appreciation for their work.

As the Dean, I am well aware of the importance of having the centers led by faculty. Since these faculty directors are the advocates for embedding more HIPs into our curriculum, their colleagues are most likely to adopt these best practices.

Another positive effect of creating these directorships has been an uptick in faculty morale all across the school. Specifically, the business faculty like having one of their peers work with them to develop a service-learning course to embed in their class more than working with an associate dean or dean to achieve this. Having the directors support their fellow faculty and encourage the embedding of HIPs in more and more business courses builds camaraderie and collegiality.

The directors of the centers also accomplish a significant amount of work each year, as is reflected in the annual evaluation of each center. Below, some of the highlights of the many contributions of each center are described in more detail.

BUSINESS, ECONOMIC, AND
APPLIED RESEARCH (BEAR)

The BEAR co-hosted the 2022 Georgia Gwinnett College Teaching, Learning, and Research Symposium on January 12–13, 2022. This academic conference was co-hosted with GGC's Center for Teaching Excellence (CTE). Built upon the success of the initial conference held January 13–14, 2021, at the 2022 conference, research by 118 authors was presented across the two-day event during virtual and in-person concurrent sessions. The authors represented 22 institutions and came from a wide range of geographic locations including

Georgia, Texas, Virginia, Maryland, Ohio, West Virginia, and Mississippi, and the countries of Peru, India, Thailand, Japan, and the United Kingdom. Presentations went through a double-blind review process.

The conference featured three tracks: general research track, SoTL research track, and an undergraduate research track. Dr. Jeff Galle and Dr. Martha "Marti" Venn, Vice Chancellor for Academic Affairs, University System of Georgia, served as the conference keynote speakers. Closing ceremony remarks were given by Regent José Perez, the Board of Regents of the University System of Georgia. GGC President Dr. Jann Joseph spoke at the keynote address and the closing ceremony, while GGC Provost Dr. George Low spoke at the opening ceremony.

The BEAR Center and CTE are now working together to plan for the 2023 conference. On a regular basis, the BEAR Center faculty also offers undergraduate research as a cross-listed course for SBA students in general and those who might want to pursue graduate studies in particular. Successful examples included students published in peer-reviewed journals (PRJs).

The BEAR is also the venue for empirical research which may have significant societal impact. Its focus lately has been on studying dual enrollment in the State of Georgia. Its findings included the amount of savings to Georgia families that participated in the program. Since tuition/cost of going to college has been one of the major challenges in higher ed, the study is both timely and informative. Most recently, the Dual Enrollment research by Drs. Wes Routon, Mark Partridge, Tracey Schaller, and Reanna Berry was featured in *Inside Higher Ed*'s Academic Minute (https://www.insidehighered .com/quicktakes/2022/05/02/dual-enrollment-pays-academic-minute).

CENTER FOR INTERNATIONAL BUSINESS AND EXCHANGE (CIBE)

The Center for International Business and Exchange (CIBE) has secured a generous grant from the Halle Foundation to send ten SBA faculty and staff to Germany for eight days during September 2022. The purpose of the trip was to explore opportunities to establish collaborative relationships with academia and industry in Germany with Berlin and Munich in particular. The expected benefits for our students are (1) enriched curricular and co-curricular activities and (2) initial study abroad program in Germany.

The CIBE also has been the hub for international exchange programs. Over the years, CIBE has developed two MOUs with two French schools, for faculty and student exchange. In 2021, during the pandemic, CIBE did a COIL session with one of the partner schools in France with French students and American students attending the session simultaneously. It has also signed a MOU with Global Solutions Institute (GSI), to help with its US Fulbright scholars' programs.

CIBE, over the years, also has been charged with SBA's study abroad program. It is designed as a faculty-led summer program, during which students visit three European countries, France, Belgium, and Switzerland, for about two weeks. During the trip, students visit major companies and organizations, e.g., Coca Cola, and NATO. During the pandemic, CIBE found an innovative way to continue the international education by designing a cross-listed course "Study-away," which invited global companies such as Walmart, Carter's, and OSF, to provide their internal operational experience virtually with our students. CIBE also supports research activities that are international in nature. For example, CIBE has been a sponsor for the AIB-SE conference for the last four years and led the SBA's participation in the X-Culture program.

CENTER FOR EMERGING BUSINESS AND ENTREPRENEURSHIP (CEBE)

By using funds generated by writing successful seed grants funded by the Provost's Office, the Center for Emerging Business and Entrepreneurship (CEBE) had a very successful start as a venue for supporting student-entrepreneurs through one-on-one mentorship. The CEBE also sponsors and its faculty director serves as a faculty advisor for a student organization, the Entrepreneur Network (TEN), which has seen its membership grow substantially. Since its inception, the most remarkable accomplishment is the CEBE's years of collaboration with Gwinnett County in designing a community-serving small business incubator that came to fruition in late 2021. After the delays due to supply-chain challenges and labor shortages, caused at least partially by the pandemic, the Gwinnett Entrepreneur Center (GEC), which is managed by the CEBE, opened its doors in December 2021. In January 2022, the onboarding process for business membership began. The GEC boasts twenty-five member-businesses, one of which is owned by a GGC student. The businesses represent a wide variety of industries including technologies, healthcare, construction, film production, health and wellness, education, and other professional and personal services. Under the direction of the CEBE faculty and staff, each business owner follows a customized graduation plan to bring their business to self-sufficiency. Beyond coaching the members, the GEC also provides entrepreneurship to the broader community. Attendance at events offered to the public exceeds 100 per month, and the center fields three to five new inquiries or requests for assistance per day on average.

Research is again a major component of the three-prong-synergy, and it plays an ongoing role in the operations of CEBE. The CEBE faculty recently published a peer-reviewed journal article documenting the development of the GEC.

LEADERSHIP AND MANAGEMENT DEVELOPMENT INSTITUTE (LMDI)

LMDI was established, again, as a hub for enhancing student engagement and success by fostering one of the HIPs, service-learning initiatives, by conducting leadership/management research, and by providing management and leadership development and training services to both internal and external stakeholders. During May through August 2021, in collaboration with GGC Human Resources, LMDI, as internal consultants, developed a leadership competency model (LCM). The LCMs are used to assess and determine attributes that are necessary for effective leadership for a wide variety of management/leadership positions in organization in general and higher education institutions in particular. This evidence-based approach outlines competencies and behaviors considered most important to the performance of GGC leadership.

Based upon the LCM, LMDI is providing leadership and management training for the newly appointed department chairs in August 2022. As a relatively new institution, GGC is transitioning to a new departmental leadership structure in AY 2022–2023. The four-day training program will serve as the initial step towards building a strong leadership capability and an empowered team of department chairs.

REFERENCE

Routon, Wes, et al. (2022). "Dual Enrollment Pays." *Inside Higher Education,* May 2, 2022. https: //www.insidehighered.com /quicktakes /2022 /05 /02 / dual-enrollment-pays-academic-minute.

Chapter 26

Reinvigorating the First Year Experience Program at Savannah State University

Frank J. Mendelson

It is not the fix-all solution—but a solid, enriching, and meaningful Freshman Experience program will be one of the greatest impactors upon retention, graduation, and developing a well-educated student.

—Professor Jonathan Lambright, Ph.D.; Interim AVP—Institutional Research, Planning and Assessment, Savannah State University

The First Year Experience (FYE) program at Savannah State University (SSU), a HBCU, has undergone continuous scrutiny and improvement over the past four years. Course redesign was undertaken in alignment with the University's strategic plan, and the *Student Success United* Quality Enhancement Plan (QEP) proposal. The result is a curriculum that provides equity across campus. Freshmen follow the same content modules and assignments; with thirty percent of the content specific to each of the four colleges.[1]

REDESIGN PROCESS OVERVIEW

Redesign and (re)launch of a program as consequential as FYE, must by necessity, include a wide set of stakeholders. Those in the academy understand the difficulty in bringing a diverse group of interests around the table on a regular, indeed a weekly basis (and occurring pre-COVID-19, the thought of using Zoom, WebEx, etc., had not even been considered). Its strength was a shared belief in the value of the program. Participation was robust.

The most substantial discussion and set of changes followed a series of ten weekly staff/faculty meetings involving upwards of twenty SSU colleagues. Many of the staff who attended had taught FYE at some point in their tenure at Savannah State; a number had taken the FYE course when attending the university as students.

SSU staff's personal history with FYE was intimate and shared an appreciation of the added value an FYE program provides. Their input helped to emphasize what worked in the past, including the need to strengthen the history and legacy modules (of HBCUs in general and SSU in specific) to foster a stronger relationship with school and immediate sense of belonging. One of the new components focuses on race, bias, diversity, equity, and inclusion. The curricular model includes five units under which instruction occurs. It was originally designed and taught by Shed Dawson.[2]

1. Connecting with College
2. Growing an Academic (Growth) Mindset
3. Developing Life Skills
4. Building an Academic Toolbox
5. Discovering Savannah State University

To earn further buy-in across the University, the committee wrote a position statement attached to the proposed curriculum revision, circulated to the four college Deans, the Provost, and VP Enrollment Management for their input and approval.[3]

First Year Experience is a high-impact practice. High-impact practices (HIPs) are active learning practices that promote deep learning by promoting student engagement as measured by the National Survey on Student Engagement (NSSE).

To be a high-impact practice, the experience must satisfy the definition established by George Kuh (2008; Kuh & O'Donnell, 2013) and his colleagues at the Association of American Colleges and Universities (AAC&U): achievement of deep learning, significant engagement gains, and positive differential impact on historically underserved student populations.[4]

Within the SSU curriculum, more HIPs are addressed, including Common Intellectual Experiences, Learning Communities, focused attention on written reflections, Collaborative Assignments and Projects, an introduction to undergraduate research, Diversity/Global Learning, and preparation for community-based learning.

FYE serves as an innovative way to continue the connection started for new students through the admission's process, as an SSU Tiger—a member of the "Tiger Nation." It is designed to help them understand the legacy of the institution and their place in that rich history while simultaneously providing them with the important skills and tools they will need to be great college students.

> The first year underpins the entire undergraduate experience. Attention to first-year students and their transition to our institutions is essential if we are to fulfill our obligation to our students and to realize our institutional potential.[5]

According to Sametria R. McFall, PhD, MPA, Assistant Vice President of Academic Affairs at Savannah State University, FYE seeks to empower students by helping them to see their place at SSU now as a student and in the future as a successful graduate and alum.

NOTES

1. FYE is a 2-credit program, with the exception of the College of Business Administration, where it is taught as a 3-credit program, with introduction to business, leadership, and professional development added for the third credit hour.

2. Shed Dawson is Director, Career Services, Leadership and Professional Development Center at Savannah State University.

3. "It is not the fix-all solution, but a solid, enriching, and meaningful Freshman Experience program will be one of the greatest impactors upon retention, graduation, and developing a well-educated student."—Professor Jonathan Lambright, Ph.D.; Interim AVP—Institutional Research, Planning and Assessment, Savannah State University

4. Based on this definition, Kuh (2013) identified ten learning experiences as high-impact practices: First Year Seminars and Experiences; Common Intellectual Experiences; Learning Communities; Writing Intensive Courses; Collaborative Assignments and Projects; Undergraduate Research; Diversity/Global Learning; Service Learning, Community-Based Learning; Internships; and Capstone Courses and Projects.

5. Mary Stuart Hunter, "Fostering student learning and success through first year programs," *Peer Review*, 8(3), 4-7.

REFERENCES

Hunter, M. S. (2006, Summer). Fostering student learning and success through first year programs. *Peer Review*, 8(3), 4-7.

Kuh, G. (2008). High-Impact educational practices: What they are, who has access to them, and why they matter. AAC&U.

Kuh, G. D., O'Donnell, K., & Reed, S. (2013). Ensuring quality and taking high-impact practices to scale. Washington DC: Association of American Colleges and Universities.

Chapter 27

The Undergraduate Research Symposium at South Georgia State College

History, Status, and Future

Robert L. Potter, Rosa Guedes, and Frank Holiwski

From small gatherings of faculty and students to day-long events on the academic calendar, the Undergraduate Research Symposium (URS) at South Georgia State College has existed in one form or another since fall 2011 and is meant to celebrate student research efforts (Holiwski & Guedes, 2019). A Faculty Learning Community (FLC) developed to organize the URS was incorporated into a Chancellor's Learning Scholar (CLS)-FLC led by Robert Potter. This paper summarizes the background, evolution, and future plans for the URS.

The FLC has three to five core members who organized the URS and preceded the CLS. The start of the Bachelors of Science in Biological Sciences program in 2013 expanded the URS, eventually evolving into a multi-day event. Now, it is a single daytime event on a Tuesday near the end of the fall and spring semesters. This past spring it was held in multiple rooms (simultaneous sessions) in a face-to-face format. Student participation were either oral presentations or posters.

Faculty participation was at three levels. In level one, students, individually or as teams, conduct research and prepare a presentation or poster. Level two has the URS incorporated into course material as a co-curricular activity. Level three offers bonus points for attendance.

Level 1 participation may require considerable modification to course material if not originally part of the course. Many courses already had student presentations as part of the course. Some of those who have participated in the URS include BIOL 2018K, PSYC 1101, POLS 1101, BIOL 3630K, BIOL 3500K, BIOL 4090K, BIOL 3130, and BIOL 4501, among others. Level 2 participation (student co-curricular activity) was encouraged to increase student involvement in the day-long URS event. This has the greatest potential to increase student involvement across disciplines on our campus. Level 3 participation (bonus points for attendance) was chosen by several faculty. While this option requires the least amount of change to a course, it too has a potential to increase student involvement. Once students participate by attending, often for bonus points, they are more likely to participate in future events.

As our school has added BS and BA programs, many of the capstone courses required classroom presentations, and there is potential for these to be incorporated into the URS structure. Several of the BS and BA chairs have expressed interest in adding their programs to future URS events. An additional component is the increasing number of internships being added to the curriculum, most of which already required presentations at some point during the year. Spring 2022 had about 230 unique student visits (12% of enrollment) and around 350 "visits" totaling all rooms and students. This approached near our pre-pandemic multi-day format numbers.

There have been over twenty different faculty members who have contributed at one of the above levels since the inception of the URS. This represents about a third of our campus faculty. This is by far the best attended of any student activity currently available on our campus, which shows a strong interest for this event by our campus community. Recent efforts include solicitation of consistent sources of funding, increased participation, and more diverse representation of subject areas. It has also been proposed to incorporate other institutions as visitors or perhaps hosts of future events.

We will keep the URS and the FLC running going forward and hope to offer our experience to any faculty who would like to add their students and themselves to this team effort.

STUDENT COMMENTS

- "The symposium allows students to conduct research and prepare a presentation over what they have learned. This opportunity has helped prepare me for graduate school and has given me experience presenting research, like I will be doing in the future."—Alana Atkinson, biology BS graduate (Currently MS program in plant pathology, UGA Tifton campus).

- "I often have stage fright when it comes to presentations, so I feel the research symposium helped me become more confident. Presentations are a part of life, so making progress on how to deal with my fears by presenting in front of an audience at the research symposium was a good experience for me."—Jared Bare, biology BS student.
- "I went on two job interviews and both of them asked me multiple questions about my experience at the research symposium—and neither of the jobs had anything to do with research, they were both in retail. I wound up taking one of those jobs, and I think talking about the symposium with the employer helped. They really seemed interested."—Travis Simons, AS psychology.
- "The symposium was very eye opening. I learned about some subjects I wouldn't otherwise seek out on my own. I will be going next semester and the next. I recommend the symposium to anyone and everyone."—Savannah Sparks, general studies.

FACULTY COMMENTS

- "They came for the points but stayed because they found something they were interested in and liked."—Dr. R. Guedes.

REFERENCE

Holiwski, F. and R. Guedes. (2019). Symposium Highlights Undergraduate Research Efforts at South Georgia State College. DouglasNow. https://www.douglasnow.com/index.php/education/item/6748-symposium-highlights-undergraduate-research-efforts-at-south-georgia-state-college

Chapter 28

New Faculty Orientation

Developing Faculty in Academic Mindsets and More

Laura R. Lynch

The College of Coastal Georgia, located in Brunswick, GA, is a four-year public college with roughly 3,200 students and 100 full-time faculty. Each year, there are 8–10 new full-time faculty, some of whom come straight from a doctoral program while others come with a wealth of teaching experience.

My position is responsible for overall faculty development, and I do that by leveraging the expertise of my colleagues across the institution in faculty development efforts while also providing space for faculty from various disciplines to collaborate on student success strategies that span disciplines. The College prides itself on student engagement, reaching every student, every time, and that begins with developing faculty as soon as they arrive at the College.

NEW FACULTY ORIENTATION

There are three main components to the collegewide new faculty orientation: a multiday pre-fall program, monthly meetings in the fall with invited speakers from around campus, and a spring semester faculty learning community that I co-lead with our COMPASS Center for Academic and Career Advising. Individual departments have additional activities for new faculty, including assigning experienced faculty to serve as mentors for new faculty.

The collegewide program has grown significantly over the last five years; through informal assessments at the end of each of the three components I make improvements each year while also adding activities based on general faculty development needs and initiatives at the institution.

The pre-fall program contains a general new employee orientation along with the key information necessary for new faculty to get started: familiarizing faculty with the institution and student body, the responsibilities of their position, and the basics of the College's learning management system. Faculty also participate in several workshops on topics covering course design, student mental health, and developing positive classroom norms. In several of these sessions, the general concept of student mindset is introduced and specific pedagogical tips shared to improve student mindset. However, faculty much like students have limited bandwidth and so we have staggered our approach to delve deeper into topics pertinent to faculty and student success throughout their first year.

In the fall semester, the focus is still on more basic information faculty need (that perhaps they just didn't need immediately). In Spring 2022, when faculty had a full semester under their belts and could devote a little more bandwidth to learning about student success strategies, we created an in-depth semester-long faculty learning community that centered on academic and career advising, both formally through an advisor-advisee relationship and informally with students in a faculty member's class and/or discipline, along with continued conversations on the importance of academic mindset in working with students. There were ten faculty participants and we look forward to continuing this program each spring. A summary of concepts covered throughout the year is shown in table 28.1.

A Focus on Mindsets

Education and psychology researchers have classified academic mindsets into four overarching categories, growth mindset, self-efficacy, sense of belonging, and purpose/value, and the research is clear that improving student academic mindsets has a lasting impact on overall student success (Farrington et al., 2012; Mindset Scholars Network, 2018).

At our institution, through survey data given to freshmen within the first few weeks of the fall semester (2017–2021), we've seen firsthand that growth mindset and sense of belonging are both positively correlated with statistical significance to grade point average. Each of the four mindset categories pairs naturally with different facets of advising (see table 28.1), which allows for us to weave into the monthly advising topics intentional discussions and examples of relevant academic mindsets and how faculty can cultivate those mindsets in their students and advisees in meaningful and relevant ways tied to interactions they already have with students. By introducing the concept of mindsets in the pre-fall workshops and then returning to the concept in the

Table 28.1. NFO Calendar of events.

Fall Semester—General Topics		Spring Semester—Advising/Mindset Focus	
September	Financial Aid and Registrar	Throughout	Participation in an advising "course" in the learning management system
Early October	COMPASS Advising and Library	February	Discussions on: Advising Basics, Campus Resources, Intrusive Advising, Growth Mindset
Late October	High-Impact Practices and IRB	March	Discussions on: Advising Technology (e.g., DegreeWorks & Student data systems), Academic Standing processes and Interventions, Self-Efficacy Mindset
November	Business Affairs and Advancement	April	Shadow an Advisor with a follow-up Advising Panel; Discussions on: Importance of Student Involvement, Sense of Belonging Mindset
December	Discussion on Annual Faculty Evaluations and General Q&A	May	Take the FOCUS2® career assessment; Discussions on: Aligning Career and Academic Goals, Career Services Resources, Purpose/Value mindset

Source: Institutional calendar of NFO events

spring with in-depth conversations that last over a full semester, grounded in something non-discipline specific (formal and/or informal advising), we are able to aid faculty in developing a deeper understanding of the importance and ubiquity of academic mindsets.

REFERENCES

Farrington, C. A., Roderick, M., Allensworth, E., Nagaoka, J., Keyes, T. S., Johnson, D. W., & Beechum, N. O. (2012). *Teaching adolescents to become learners. The role of noncognitive factors in shaping school performance: A critical literature review*. Chicago: University of Chicago Consortium on Chicago School Research.

Mindset Scholars Network. (2018). Leveraging mindset science to design learning environments that nurture people's natural drive to learn. http://studentexperiencenetwork.org/wp-content/uploads/2018/01/Learning-Enviros-Research-Brief.pdf.

Chapter 29

Developing Expertise for Teaching through a Graduate Fellows Program

Ania Kowalik

As an educational developer at a research-intensive university, I regularly work with graduate students eager to develop teaching expertise that is often missing from the training provided by their departments. In the summer of 2021, I redesigned our Graduate Fellows program to better reflect the needs and goals of our students. As a small, modestly resourced Center, our Fellows dedicate only thirty hours per academic year to the fellowship, which limits the scope of their work. Given these challenges, I asked two guiding questions when redesigning the program:

1. What high-impact activities can be embedded into this program to foster the development of teaching expertise?
2. How to provide mentorship and feedback opportunities within the time Fellows dedicate to the fellowship?

TEACHING EXPERTISE IN GRADUATE DEVELOPMENT

In higher education, teaching expertise is characterized by pedagogical content knowledge (an understanding of how particular content can best be taught to a novice learner), professional learning (a growth-mindset approach to developing teaching expertise), and "the artistry of teaching" (a term referring to the non-routine, intuitive, and improvisational nature of teaching) (King, 2022).

All these elements are embedded into our Graduate Fellows program. During their fellowship, each Fellow commits to developing and facilitating one 90-minute workshop and attends regular planning and feedback sessions with other Fellows. Since each cohort includes 3–4 Fellows, these expectations fit within the time Fellows allocate to the fellowship.

The workshop is a pedagogical event that offers Fellows ample opportunities for developing all elements of teaching expertise:

- **Pedagogical content knowledge**: When developing workshop agenda and activities Fellows have to ask themselves the same questions they would ask in a real classroom context: What are my learning goals? What is the best way to organize the session to meet those goals? How to introduce this topic to novice learners? What are the best activities to engage the participants? How can I assess whether I have met my goals?
- **The artistry of teaching**: The workshop provides some exposure to the unpredictable nature of the classroom. During their workshops Fellows had to troubleshoot the activities that generated too few ideas or too robust a discussion for the time allowed. They had to deal with low participation and adjust workshop activities accordingly. They had to tackle questions they didn't know how to answer. All these called for creativity, thinking on the spot, and resilience demanded of all educators.
- **Professional learning**: Regular workshop planning and feedback sessions allowed students to reflect on their design choices, draft and revise workshop agendas, provide feedback and support to their peers, and share pedagogical ideas across disciplinary contexts. These sessions fostered a reflective approach to teaching and encouraged a collaborative, community-based environment for developing teaching expertise.

PROGRAM DESIGN

The limited time and resources posed their own design challenges for me. The three following solutions allowed me to create a few efficiencies without compromising the learning experience for the students:

1. **Transparency about the process and expectations.** I provided clear criteria for developing workshop objectives, activities, and assessments to ensure that each workshop is interactive. This approach helped with the design process as well as peer feedback.
2. **Using a self-paced approach with exemplars where possible.** In addition to clear guidelines, I also provided exemplars of annotated workshop agendas and handouts to help students through the design

process. These resources helped Fellows develop high-quality materials and made the peer feedback more efficient.

3. **Designing for peer feedback.** As a high-impact practice, peer feedback allowed students to be thoughtful and intentional about the learning design process, adding to their learning experience in the program. It also helped every Fellow remain invested in each workshop throughout the duration of the fellowship.

DOES IT WORK?

While more data is needed to determine the effectiveness of the program, early feedback from the first cohort of Fellows suggests that it helped them strengthen key pedagogical competencies such as deepening the knowledge of learning theories, setting and communicating learning goals, teaching with the attention to diversity and inclusion, and improving the ability to use evidence-based approaches (Gilmore & Hatcher, 2021).

One student also shared that she relied on her experience designing and facilitating the workshop to talk about her preparation for teaching during an academic job interview. This feedback suggests that Future Faculty programs, even those with modest resources, can help fill an urgent need in graduate student professional development.

REFERENCES

Gilmore, J. and Hatcher, M. (Eds.). (2021). *Preparing for college and university teaching: Competencies for graduate and professional students.* Sterling.

King, H. (2022). The characteristics of expertise for teaching in higher education. In H. King (Ed.), *Developing expertise for teaching in higher education: Practical ideas for professional learning and development* (pp. 15–28). Routledge.

Chapter 30

The New Faculty Academy of the Center for Teaching Excellence

Miranda M. Zhang

The Center for Teaching Excellence (CTE) at Georgia Gwinnett College (GGC), a teaching-intensive institution, focuses on providing programming that promotes the design and implementation of successful learning environments for the faculty in achieving the goal of student success.

In particular, the center provides programs that highlight student engagement and the development of innovative teaching and learning strategies. In doing so, the center fosters a culture that values college teaching and learning as vital forms of scholarship to increase student success by improving the quality of teaching across academic programs. We support and facilitate several collaborative faculty learning communities that practice and recognize innovative and effective instruction in academic programs.

One of the notable pedagogical programming is the annual New Faculty Academy (NFA) that provides a yearlong onboarding experience for new GGC faculty. The primary purpose is to improve the way new faculty are prepared for their teaching, research, and service responsibilities at the institution. The program is designed to welcome and help support the newest members of the full-time faculty who are in their first year of academic responsibilities in different schools and disciplines.

The goals of the NFA program include the following:

- Increase understanding, broaden perspectives, and develop the skills of new GGC faculty.
- Increase understanding of the changing role of GGC faculty.
- Increase understanding of the changes taking place in teaching and learning.

Depending on each year's number of new faculty members and the disciplines, the program can be scheduled on a monthly or weekly basis with various pedagogical contents. The workshops focus on sharing and developing essential skills that faculty need to successfully navigate the early years of their research and teaching careers. There is a strong emphasis on implementing active learning strategies in the classroom. The workshops are designed to be interactive in nature with content—teaching, scholarship, or service—that can be applied immediately.

Onsite, participants can discuss any content related questions as well as ask academic professional development questions. Beside the members of the Center for Teaching Excellence, extensive expertise from other areas on campus are invited to facilitate the workshops, including the library, student engagement and success division, and the faculty fellows in integrative learning and experiential learning.

Examples of recent workshop subjects include the following:

- Library resources for faculty
- Student engagement and success resources
- Mentoring and advising resources
- Course design methods
- Integrative learning/teaching
- Creating accessible content
- Work/life balance and the "reflective practitioner" session
- Formative assessment (two series)
- How to develop a SoTL project
- Experiential learning/teaching
- Sponsored research and program resources

Each year, nearly 100% of new faculty members participated in and benefited from the program. The feedback from the survey indicates the NFA is a very worthwhile and successful program in helping to support the new faculty to begin their academic responsibilities at their new institution with stronger key pedagogical competencies and confidence.

Chapter 31

Interprofessional Education Collaborative

A Pilot Project

Laura Kim Gosa

WHAT IS IPE?

Interprofessional Education (IPE) is vital in curriculum innovation design to enable healthcare students the ability to learn by connecting between their own disciplines of study and the knowledge of other disciplines. This offers an enriched educational experience and prepares the student to provide safe, effective, and efficient healthcare to patients and meet the needs of a complex healthcare system (McNaughton, 2018).

Health education has traditionally been delivered to a discipline specific student which requires lecture and clinical experiences. However, the healthcare workplace is complex and requires different professions to work together, within and across team settings.

IMPORTANCE, GOALS/MISSION, & EXPECTATIONS

The idea was to create interdisciplinary simulation to bring an innovative teaching strategy to students, while collaborating across disciplines at ASU, and to partner with a local health system to facilitate the pilot project event to engage students in a learning simulation experience. Faculty across various disciplines have been engaged in the planning of this pilot program in hopes to develop a robust program, specifically when our new simulation center is completed.

Additionally, this project idea was formed when the COVID-19 pandemic manifested numerous challenges to how healthcare faculties can foster clinical learning experiences to health and nursing students across ASU as students were prohibited from attending onsite clinical learning during the heightened pandemic periods.

New innovative methods needed to be developed; therefore, the project was created by this author. Although the virus had negative impacts to faculty, students, and the shifting to online learning, positive aspects/ideas and learning transpired as well. This prompted faculty to become creative to construct clinical experiences using simulation experiences. They worked with other professional disciplines to foster a "real-life" simulation scenario and bring theory from the classroom to help facilitate interdisciplinary learning with disciplines from the Physical & Occupation Therapy Assistant program and the Nursing, Respiratory Therapy, and Case Management departments to improve and enhance educational experiences beyond an individual skill competence to a collectively competent patient-centered team at ASU.

BENEFITS TO FACULTY & STUDENTS

This project is vital to healthcare because good team functioning is associated with good patient outcomes, increased staff satisfaction, and quality of patient care (Reitsma et al., 2019). This pilot project will lay the groundwork for more advanced learning activities and can improve patient outcomes and will enhance team-based learning when ASU's Simulation Center is completed. The mission of the project is to facilitate interprofessional educational opportunities and academic-practice partnerships among healthcare faculty, professionals, and students at Albany State University.

The benefits to students are to establish four interprofessional competency domains for collaborative practice: values and ethics, roles and responsibilities, interprofessional communication, and teamwork. The project addresses student success based on the four goals of ASU's Strategic plan: (1) facilitating student success to enter workforce in healthcare, (2) empowering sustainability and stewardship to enhance learning across disciplines and promote a team environment to educate health students and to increase enrollments, (3) partnering with a local healthcare facility to foster student learning and promote competitiveness with ASU's dynamic force of healthcare professions being offered to our students, and (4) promoting faculty development and leadership development to facilitate learning together and being a part of a purpose to engage multiple areas of ASU to foster interprofessional educational learning to our students.

REFERENCES

McNaughton, S. (2018). The long-term impact of undergraduate interprofessional education on graduate interprofessional practice: A scoping review. *Journal of Interprofessional Care, 32*(4), 426–435.

Reitsma, G., Scrooby, B., Rabie, T., Vijoen, M., Smit, K., Du Preez, A., Pretorius, R., Van Oort, A., Swanepoel, M., Naude, A., and Dolman, R. (2019). Health students' experiences of the process of interprofessional education: A pilot project. *Journal of Interprofessional Care, 33*(3), 298–307.

PART III

Pedagogies of Engagement
and the Curriculum

Chapter 32

Innovating the General Education Program, Programs of Study, and New Degrees

Jeffery Galle and Jo Galle

As previously demonstrated with course redesign and program enrichment, the eight sets of learning strategies called the pedagogies of engagement, when integrated with the right fit into courses and programs, can enrich the learning opportunities for students in the courses and programs. These pedagogies of engagement are the teaching moves that faculty can make to connect students to disciplinary or program content through individual engagement and experience.

The primary function of the eight sets of learning strategies is to establish multiple bridges from individual response to the disciplines, the courses, and the various programs. The primary reason for doing this is that these bridges are precisely the way individuals learn. And these points of entry, these bridges to introductory course content, can also be employed to deepen student learning across the entire curriculum.

To shift the metaphor from the bridge, it could be said, with these larger academic structures—the General Education Program (GEP), new degree program proposals, and the undergraduate curriculum—the pedagogies of engagement can become the honey or spice to attract and to enliven the learning experience of students.

An example of how importance given to the experience of the learner is occurring at the uppermost system level is at the University System of Georgia's Board of Regents, where its academic affairs leaders have added new questions to the New Degree Application Form. Now, there are questions requiring institutions to identify specific High-Impact Practices (HIPs) that are woven into the degree plan.[1] The same application form requires institutions to further explain how the specific HIPs will influence degree outcomes. An institution's just listing several of the AACU's HIPs is considered an insufficient answer, and instead, it must be demonstrated that these HIPs and practices must be woven into the proposed degree.

Experiential learning, individual response, multiple points of entry—these are the hallmarks of good courses, programs, and yes, the curriculum itself. In a well-known guide to General Education revision, Paul Gaston and Jerry Gaff point to several positive influences on general education reform. They note, it is "widely shared that students learn most readily by becoming actively involved in their own education."[2]

From the perspective of what faculty provide, Gaston and Gaff talk about the importance of strategies and practices. "There is broad agreement that a curriculum is only as effective as the pedagogy that supports it."[3] Hence, if the curricular structures are treated like an individual course, then the questions presented in earlier chapters to develop learning in courses should be the same with new degrees, general education, and the curriculum.

What is an overarching idea that can galvanize mindset, student interest, assignments, research projects, and the classroom activities? What is, for example, the corollary for the exploration of the canon in a literary studies course when we seek a golden thread for the curricular structures?

The answer will rightly vary from institution to institution, because the identity of each can provide that overarching idea, and, of course, institutions also vary by sector, from the research university to the state university, or the state college. Andrew Delbanco undertakes to "articulate what a college— any college—should seek to do for its students." While he is also well aware of the prevalence of the patterns set early on by Harvard, Yale, Princeton, and a few others, Delbanco aimed to identify the common or shared responsibility of all institutions.[4]

If the search for an overarching idea or a uniqueness of the particular institution is blended with elements of pedagogical innovation and also includes a special focus on pedagogy, practices, and student engagement across the campus, then the learning outcomes of the students will be fine, whatever the particular fascinating identity or history the institution possesses.

At Oxford College of Emory University, the Ways of Inquiry is the thread that defines the general education experience for students at this premier college, offering the first two years of study toward an Emory University baccalaureate. As a school within one of the world's top ranked research institutions, to thread the elements of the student learning experience with Inquiry, or specifically, ways that inquiry is undertaken within individual disciplines, makes perfect sense.[5]

By Ways of Inquiry or INQ, is meant a disciplinary way of doing work within the discipline, constructing knowledge, and essentially conducting research. Hence, every discipline has its own way of knowing. Students across the first two years of study enroll in a number of these INQ courses and develop a knowledge and appreciation of the different ways of inquiry.

INQUIRY WITH THE MEMOIR AND LITERARY CRITICISM

In each Ways of Inquiry course, students learn something of the disciplinary work of the course's discipline, perhaps how to conduct research/inquiry in the discipline, and to themselves produce an artifact of disciplinary work.

Literary studies offer a number of specialty areas, each of which possesses its own research interests and questions as well as its own scholarly products. At Oxford College, an INQ course on the Memoir is a literature course that is also a writing course. Students will undertake the study of four or five professional memoirs, and also read critical essays on issues within the Memoir as a genre, issues and questions that arise in the writing of a memoir, and various ongoing debates that scholars have.

With most of these materials, the Memoir course works like a traditional writing and readings course with a set number of pages to be read for discussion in each class meeting, a number of multiple draft essays, a couple of written exams, daily quizzes, class activities, student conferences, and student-led facilitation of discussion.

What makes the INQ class unique is students are challenged to create a product like those they are reading, essentially a memoir-like paper not of book length, but a long essay that meets the criteria of the memoir as genre. This assignment creates great excitement, because the students are essentially writing their own lives or central moments of their life. The assignment becomes the culmination of their study of the memoir, so it's completed at the semester's end. Students can share it with other students if they like. Some students want to do their research presentation on their memoir essay.

In the Literary Criticism course, many pedagogical elements of the course are similar to the Memoir course—set number of pages to discuss each class meeting, multiple essays each in multiple drafts, a set of readings on literary criticism and its schools of interpretation or approaches to interpretation, quizzes, research project, and presentation.

The unique product for students in this course is they will write a literary interpretation of a very new short story, only recently published so without a critical, interpretive history.[6] They will produce work within the discipline just as a literary critic produces. Similar to writing the memoir essay, the writing of a literary interpretation (using one or more of the critical lenses that the class has studied) really generates a great deal of excitement.

In both courses, students adopt a particular professional stance in addressing questions a memoirist must consider or in selecting and applying the elements of the critical school to the short story at hand. In brief then, Oxford College's General Education Program, its Ways of Inquiry, asks students to think like the disciplinary experts and in so doing, to produce something similar to what experts produce.

The underlying reason for creating a particular General Education Program (GEP) should be much more than a menu of courses. If a feature unites the GEP, then general education becomes an actual program that dovetails into the curriculum, perhaps connects to institutional identity and aspiration for students, while it builds the knowledge, skills, and attitudes needed for students to become active citizens of a democracy.

Can this work be done at the system level? Perhaps, but that effort will be very difficult because institutions tend to want something unique for themselves. Perhaps it is more easily achieved if the system develops a system wide GEP as a blend of requisite courses and some freedom to define the uniqueness much like research institutions like Emory focused on inquiry.

The shift from the GEP to the undergraduate curriculum can be an integrated shift from a thoughtfully designed GEP into programs of study across the institution. In its simplest terms, a curriculum is the set of courses required of students for completion of the degree, but as we have argued with courses, programs, and the GEP, this set of courses can be so much more than a mere list.

For an institution, the programs of study begin with identity and values, moves into the content that embodies that identity and institutional values, and ends up being part of what each student carries away from the institution and forward.

For an individual faculty enacting innovative strategies and activities within all of his or her classes may be the full representation of "putting it all together." Similarly, for a department or division, the representation of innovation and engagement across the entire division may involve scores of faculty courses and thousands of students. When the entire institution is involved in a student learning project or initiative, the scale increases exponentially.

The primary focus of *Putting It All Together* has been the teaching moves that faculty and even staff can make to engage students in learning. Looked at in this way, a program of study joins what a professional in a specific career knows, can do skillfully, and has specific attitudes that carry him or her forward. The career, the position, the job—all meet innovative pedagogy and student learning in this effort.

At Georgia College and State University, the four-year undergraduate curriculum is called Journeys, or GC Journeys. Experiential learning across the undergraduate program is the golden thread, and the eleven High-Impact Practices of the AACU provide the substance of the experiential learning experiences that enrich courses at Georgia College. This curriculum is the subject of the next chapter and is authored by the Georgia College leader, Jordan Cofer, whose responsibilities include transformative learning.

John Tagg recognized Learning Paradigm institutions as those that have replaced an institutional paradigm with an *instructional* paradigm which possesses several pronounced features: supporting students in pursuing their goals, offering frequent student performances, providing frequent and ongoing feedback, providing intrinsic motivation, and possessing stable communities of practice.[7]

In a similar way, this book presents the argument for faculty, staff, and administrators, indeed, for entire institutions, to begin within individual context and work to create enriched learning opportunities for every student in that context. Beginning within an individual context, each professional undertakes thoughtful transformation of academic content by bringing mindset strategies, inclusive practices, inquiry, experiential learning practices, and active classrooms that spark student learning as the topmost value.

NOTES

1. The work of Marti Venn and her team at the University System of Georgia's System Office redesigned the New Degree Proposal form to include items on HIPs that every institution in the USG applying for a new degree must respond to in detail.

2. Paul L. Gaston and Jerry G. Gaff, *Revising General Education* (Washington DC: American Association of American Colleges and Universities, 2009), 3. They also cite George Kuh, *High-Impact Educational Practices: What They Are, Who Has Access to Them, and Why They Matter* (AAC&U, 2008) as one of the primary authorities for this developing attitude towards student learning.

3. Gaston and Gaff, 3.

4. Andrew Delbanco, *College: What It Was, Is, and Should Be* (Princeton: Princeton University Press, 2012), 6–8. Around the time he published this book, I was privileged to have dinner with Delbanco and the campus dean of Oxford College. Delbanco's teaching at Columbia, the frame for his talk to Oxford College faculty, and the evening conversation at dinner, centered on the commonalities that we share.

5. Virginia S. Lee worked with Oxford College faculty in a number of college workshops as well as within multiple years of the Institute for Pedagogy in the Liberal Arts at Oxford College. Her edited collection *Teaching and Learning Through Inquiry* (Stylus, 2004) was very important in faculty discussions as Ways of Inquiry GEP developed.

6. An anthology of short stories like *One World: A Global Anthology of Short Stories* (ed. Chris Brazier, New Internationalist, 2009) was very useful source for new stories without a critical history. Also, anthologies of Best American Stories annually published is another good resource.

7. John Tagg, *The Learning Paradigm College* (San Francisco: Anker Publishing, 2003).

Chapter 33

Putting It Together

GC Journeys

Jordan Cofer

In 2018–2019, Georgia College launched *GC Journeys*, a signature initiative focused on high-impact practices (HIPs) that was years in the making. By working with faculty, collaborating on the initiative development, engaging the campus, supporting innovation, and measuring success, institutions can build a similar institutional-based initiative.

GC Journeys asks all Georgia College students to complete five HIPs during their undergraduate program of study, while also embedding the AAC&U Essential Learning Outcomes into the curriculum. On campus, we branded our HIPs as "Transformative Experiences" and our Essential Learning Outcomes as "Essential Skills" (see figure 33.1).

For GC Journeys to work, and for any institution to offer HIPs at scale, faculty development has to be at the forefront. At Georgia College, faculty were architects of the initiative, starting with a faculty team who, after attending the AAC&U High-Impact Practices Summer Institute, came back to campus and formed a cohort. This cohort ultimately led to the creation of our GC Journeys initiative.

While all areas of campus are involved in GC Journeys, much of the pedagogical support comes from the Center for Teaching and Learning (CTL). The CTL offers a summer High-Impact Practices Institute for twenty faculty to learn about and design a high-impact practice. This is a competitive program for which faculty apply each year. We also offer monthly information sessions, two separate 90-minute workshops (High-Impact Practices and Essential Learning Outcomes), and workshops on various HIPs. The CTL runs multiple HIPs Faculty Learning Communities and has offered a multi-week course for faculty. Finally, the Center for Teaching and Learning

Deep Learning Experiences by Cumulative Participation in High-Impact Practices (HIPs)

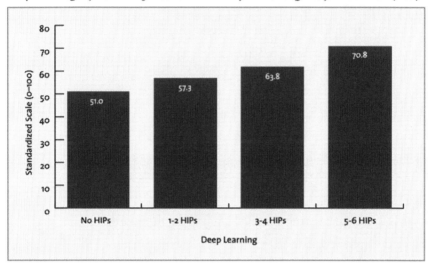

Figure 33.1.   Deep learning experiences by number of HIPs. *Source: Finley and McNair (2013), p. 10.*

gathered a group of faculty experts to design "Faculty Success Frameworks," a type of rubric for each high-impact practice.

GC Journeys also offers financial support for faculty leading HIPs in the form of small project "mini-grants." These have varied between department mini-grants for an individual department or program and project mini-grants to support individual experiences.

At first, the biggest challenges for GC Journeys revolved around scaling and tracking the HIPs. With GC Journeys, each department submitted a plan of how they would integrate HIPs into their curriculum. Meanwhile, the Director of GC Journeys worked with each department on this plan to ensure that all students have an embedded capstone experience. The Associate Provost and the Registrar worked closely with department chairs to create a curricular "tagging" system. For a HIP to "count," it must receive a "course tag," and to receive a tag, it must meet the operational definitions, which were written by faculty. To help, GC Journeys created resources for faculty and chairs to work together to assure the experiences are "high-impact." While these processes work well, it is also important to consistently update and double-check quality standards on HIPs.

Another challenge that has arisen in developing an innovative program like GC Journeys is that it is difficult to find a computer program that can handle tracking the experiences for students. Finally, a more recent challenge that has emerged from our program assessments is that students don't always "speak the language," so it is necessary to work with all stakeholders to be sure that we are educating students about the experiences that they are engaging in.

The end result has been a truly transformative approach to pedagogy. Ultimately, designing the initiative with tracking and assessing in mind, has made the initiative easier to sustain long term. As our HIPs Assessment data from the Indiana University HIPs Quality Study has shown, our high-impact practices are being offered at and sometimes above the national scale (see figure 33.2).

Undergraduate Research

	High experiences for performance	Demand time & effort	Substantive interaction w/faculty & peers	They help students engage across differences	They provide students with rich feedback	Structured opportunity to reflect & integrate	Opportunity to apply & test learning in new situations	Public demonstration of competence
National	++	++	++		+	+	++	++
GC	++	++	++		+	++	++	++

Figure 33.2. Comparative data on Undergraduate Research. *Source: Indiana University HIPs Quality Study, 2020.*

The end result has created a university wide initiative with stakeholders across the campus. GC Journeys has won both statewide and national awards for curricular innovation. However, what we are most proud of is how it has impacted our students. It has helped raise retention and student engagement, and our students recognize these experiences as transformative (see figure 33.3).

GC Journeys At A Glance
GC Journeys Participation Data

Experience	2018-2019	2019-2020	2020-2021	2021-2022	Difference
First Year Experience	1642	1519	1537	1684	+147
Career Milestones	452	324	520	826	+306
Capstone	1053	1118	1021	1287	+266
Leadership	584	602	776	792	+16
Undergrad Research	1318	2325	1737	2437	+700
CbEL	477	728	466	297	-169
Internships	1076	1086	962	1420	+458
Study Abroad	255	203	3	23	+20
Total Student Participation	6857	7905	7022	8766	+1744

Figure 33.3. GC Journeys Participation Data. *Source: GC Journeys Participation Data (Fall 2018–Spring 2022).*

PART IV

Putting It All Together

Chapter 34

An Exaltation of Larks

Jeffery Galle

The image and the sound of an exaltation of larks at dawn of a new day is a beautiful metaphor for the unified collective effort of many different individuals moving together toward a common goal.[1]

When every professional—faculty, staff, and administrator—intentionally places student learning as their top priority within the contexts where their work engages with students, then everyone can work within distinct but overlapping areas for the same purpose. When, moreover, that priority takes the form of courses, programs, and curricula enriched by pedagogies and practices that put student learning first, then higher education institutions will have the means to address Derek Bok's criticism of being underachieving.[2]

Engagement by design, by classroom activities, by student experiences in the field, and by the transparent work that students undertake—these are the contexts within which the learning moves occur.

The knowledge, skills, and attitudes foundational to academic, disciplinary, and work success are unlocked by the pedagogies and practices of mindset, inclusion, and experiential learning through the High-Impact Practices (HIPs); feedback and assessment techniques in each classroom; and classroom practices that are suited to learning both individually and within a group. What this means in practice then is in every context, every program, the first question to answer is what will our students be learning, and how will that learning make them stronger members of the academic community?

What all share is the focus on student learning and resulting success. Some will develop early alert programs—interventions such as those devised by Tim Renick at Georgia State University, for example. Before the advent of early alert and other interventions, Dr. Renick initiated a number of creative ideas like small student grants, creation of data files to track student progress, and professional advisors. Some will develop better advising programs, co-curricular programs, enriched courses, institutes, and curricula. Each professional is unique to her role and expertise, yet each also possess the same goal.

Put simply, each professional working separately but pulling toward the common goal by investing each course, program, and the curriculum with the materials that support student success writ large and within the major, the discipline—this is the essence of "putting it all together."

Teaching moves, the pedagogies of engagement, enrich learning opportunities in courses where faculty have adopted and embedded them, and the same can be true for programs and the larger curricular features of the General Education Program (GEP) and the undergraduate curriculum.

Limiting the good to those who have adopted the practices is fundamentally short sighted. Rather, a more forward-looking approach is to design all courses, programs, and even the curriculum with student learning given as much of a priority as the content that students must acquire. Telling them versus showing them how to learn is the difference between night and day.

With this goal in mind, there are a number of possible tasks or activities that can be undertaken by leaders within each context. Beginning with a state's system office as the context with the greatest reach, the editors provide a series of can-do lists for successive contexts through institutional leadership, to deans and directors, faculty, and staff. What can I do as a faculty member, as a program leader or director, as staff, as dean, or provost?

What follows is a set of possibilities for each member of the community arranged from the broadest authority through campus leadership, to the individual faculty.

THE STATE SYSTEM OFFICE OR BOARD OF REGENTS

1. The university system office can create a Toolkit for all faculty and explore the Toolkit across programs, GEP, and curricula and new courses. Such a toolkit could be produced by a state committee of pedagogical scholars and prize-winning faculty. If one exists, the group of directors of the state's teaching and learning centers would be a talented group who could produce such a Toolkit with wide appeal and institutional endorsement. In Georgia, this group is the state's Teaching and Learning Consortium.
2. Another resource to emphasize is establishing a Faculty Learning Community (FLC) program that is systemwide as was done in the University System of Georgia. Doing so with the highest fidelity to quality will mean creating a program that ensures each pedagogy of engagement will be done well.

INSTITUTIONAL LEADERSHIP: PROVOST OFFICE

The Provost or Senior Vice President can engage in the following:

1. Extend efforts to revise tenure and promotion policies that reward teaching excellence for pre- and post-tenured faculty.
2. Extend and strengthen efforts to meaningfully connect academics to campus life where they can strengthen student learning and success.
3. Create an institutional FLC program dedicated to outcomes similar to the USG's CLS program.
4. Explore possibilities of developing an institutional program like an institute for faculty development or an event that supports growth of a particular HIP such as an undergraduate student research conference, for example, that can define priorities of the institution and develop that identity.
5. Explore developing a HIPs institution-wide program such as an institutional First Year Experience program, a Service Learning Program, or an Undergraduate Research Program. Some universities have found significant advantages in developing an ePortfolio program. HIPs done well are proven to deepen learning; scaling that impact makes sense.
6. Prioritize growth and support of the institution's teaching and learning center. The POD Teaching Center Matrix is a good one to use.[3]
7. Place student learning within the context of course enrichment and redesign for all courses.

DEANS AND DIRECTORS

1. For deans, examine tenure and promotion policy and post-tenure policy to prioritize and reward faculty for excellence in teaching. Provide a number of methods for evaluating excellence, to include but not limited to student evaluations, qualitative assessments, and peer evaluations.
2. Create a process for course and program redesign and enrichment.
3. Embed student learning/success materials, particularly mindset, inclusion, and HIPs, within the program, program docs, processes, and assessment approaches of the program.
4. Discern what next step can be taken to connect the program to its counterparts on campus, nationally, and regionally.
5. Identify outlets/venues for presentations/research findings of the program. This may include developing a research plan for the program. Engage in data gathering and regular analyses of data.

6. Offer to collaborate with academic affairs or departments within the institution on matters where the potential for "divine comity" is possible.
7. Urge participation in faculty learning communities that explore student learning pedagogy. In some cases, the administrators' facilitation of the FLC may be beneficial.

INDIVIDUAL FACULTY

1. Embed in individual courses the student learning pedagogies; the eight primary ones of this book are central. Consider the overarching idea of each course, the coordinated fit of classroom activities, the selection of appropriate High-Impact Practices, and the arc of student work across the course.
2. Revise one's personal teaching statement and teaching philosophy to reflect a deep focus on student learning and reflective approach to teaching. This may involve balancing devotion to the discipline and that original passion to communicate excitement for the discipline with more knowledge of how students learn and ways to bring more students into the community of the discipline.
3. Serve as a FLC facilitator, a leadership role that calls for fostering the belonging of individual faculty into a small community of colleagues. As the FLC facilitator, avoid lecture and encourage each participant to enter the focused conversation, and use a servant leadership model to simulate how learning can occur in the learning community and in the classroom.
4. Advocate for and lead discussion of updating both the Tenure and Promotion policy and the Post-Tenure Review process. Both documents can prioritize teaching as the topmost priority for securing tenure and having successful post-tenure reviews.
5. Mentor new and other faculty both informally and also formally when a more formal arrangement is available. The mentoring can prioritize teaching strategies and practices, particularly those reviewed in this book.
6. Advocate for General Education Program review and updates, particularly in the areas of enriched courses, and review all with a view to the student's perspective and experience.
7. Advocate for adoption of appropriate pedagogies of engagement by student success programs in the institution, and offer expertise in developing necessary knowledge and skill in practitioners.

8. Conduct and publish Scholarship of Teaching and Learning experiments in classes, in collaboration with other colleagues, and in support of state or system initiatives.

Ultimately, faculty's passion for their discipline is a two-edged sword: it both opens the discipline to those who are prepared/ready and closes the discipline (or erects unnecessary barriers) to the rest of the students. So for us to address Bok's criticism, it is imperative we understand that how we engage students in our courses, programs, and curricula is more fundamental to deepening their learning than exposure to the content itself.

There is so much more to our roles as faculty, staff, and leaders of all types. We are disciplinary experts with research and service responsibilities. Both service and research are significant areas of responsibility generally outside of the scope of the teaching focus of this book. With that said, when student learning becomes the institutions top priority, and by excellent teaching we mean deeper learning, then all departments across the institution share a common metric for success. And more importantly, they can now share a common vocabulary for what constitutes success.

THE UNIVERSAL MECHANISM: A FACULTY LEARNING COMMUNITY PROGRAM

Thus far, across many framing chapters and examples from contributors, we have assumed a working knowledge of the faculty learning community. We have focused on the content rather than the mechanism that enables institutions to scale innovation across an entire institution. Now, posted below is a brief discussion of the successful faculty learning community program process.

Selection of facilitators and their in-depth workshopping of selected topics are key first steps. The steps that follow the confirmation of facilitators include establishing the timeline and the number of meetings, settling on the anticipated products of course changes and annual reports from each learning community upon completion of the year, and commitment of the resourcing necessary for support of a learning community program.

Selection of the facilitators involves finding a good fit of an applicant to the goals and outcomes of the FLC program.[4] In turn, good facilitators who exhibit this good fit can also benefit from specific workshopping in facilitation of conversation, in-depth training in pedagogical topics, and managing a timeline that works for everyone. If done well, FLC efforts can produce significant innovations in every context, which for this book has been courses, programs, and the curriculum.

Bringing about student learning is the guiding principle of selection of the content of the learning community program. Equipping faculty, staff, and administrators with this knowledge and skills will give them a common tool-kit[5] and do more to ensure institutional growth toward what all should aspire to and what John Tagg characterized as being vibrant "learning paradigm institutions."[6]

As one example, the most recent iteration of learning communities, the Chancellor's Learning Scholar's program, began by asking provosts to submit a limited number of nominated faculty, who were then invited to submit a letter of application. Upon confirmation of those selected, a cohort of facilitators was formed. These leading faculty were given multiple workshops on pedagogical topics and formed an online network using email the first year and a website platform by the second year. Each was given the prestigious title, Chancellor's Learning Scholar, and led an intra-institutional learning community for two successive years.

The system office academic affairs faculty developers and the state's teaching directors provided regular check-ins for facilitators. From selection, through formation of individual communities, the regular check-ins, and the production of annual reports cataloging hundreds of course changes and improvements, the process grew more refined with each year. A number of system experiments were conducted, and many individual members conducted their own course experiments.

NOTES

1. James Lipton, *An Exaltation of Larks* (New York: Penguin Books, 1993).
2. Bok has argued "The bad news is that most of the problems are not being seriously addressed on campuses today, nor will they be until they are correctly identified and clearly understood by those responsible for the quality of teaching and learning in our colleges (*Our Underachieving Colleges* [Princeton University Press, 2006], 10).
3. file:///C:/Users/Jeff/Downloads/ACE-PODTeachingCenterMatrix2018.pdf. Accessed November 2022.
4. Milton Cox created the founding model of the advantages afforded by a program of learning communities.
5. The Toolkit was a feature of the FLC program in the USG, thanks to the creativity of Dr. Denise Domizi and the consortium of teaching center directors. The Toolkit itself was TiLTed to possess Purpose, Tasks, and Criteria, and the content became the resource that scholar facilitators across the state's twenty-six institutions used and commonly referred to. We also could introduce each new cohort to the Toolkit at the beginning of each year's work.
6. John Tagg, *The Learning Paradigm College* (San Francisco: Anker Publishing, 2003) is the source of this idea of an institution devoted to learning.

Bibliography

Bain, Ken. *Super Courses: The Future of Teaching and Learning.* (Princeton: Princeton University Press, 2021).

Blessinger, Patrick, ed. *Inquiry-Based Learning for Faculty and Institutional Development.* (Bingley, UK: Emerald Publishing, 2014).

Bok, Derek. *Our Underachieving Colleges: A Candid Look at How Much Students Learn and Why They Should be Learning More.* (Princeton: Princeton University Press, 2006).

Boyer 2030 Commission Report. *The Equity/Excellence Imperative: A 2030 Blueprint for Undergraduate Education at U.S. Research Universities.* Online: https://ueru .org/boyer2030.

Brazier, Chris, ed. *One World: A Global Anthology of Short Stories.* (New Internationalist, 2009).

Chambliss, Daniel and Christophre Takacs. *How College Works.* (Harvard University Press, 2014).

Christakis, Nicholas and James Fowler, *Connected: The Surprising Power of Our Social Networks and How They Shape Our Lives.* (San Francisco: Back Bay Books, 2011).

Cook, James and Christopher Lewis, eds. *Student and Academic Affairs Collaboration: The Divine Comity.* (Washington, DC: National Association of Student Personnel, 2007).

Darby, Flower. *Small Teaching Online: Applying Learning Science in Online Classes.* (San Francisco: Jossey Bass, 2019).

Delbanco, Andrew. *College: What It Was, Is, and Should Be.* (Princeton: Princeton University Press, 2012).

Dweck, C. S. Mindset: *The New Psychology of Success.* (Random House, 2006).

Felten, Peter and Leo M. Lambert. *Relationship-Rich Education: How Human Connections Drive Success in College.* (Baltimore: Johns Hopkins Press, 2020).

Finley, Ashley, & Tia McNair. *Assessing Underserved Students' Engagement in High Impact Practices.* (AC&U Publications, 2013).

Frontier Set Annual Conference 2020. *Realizing Transformation Together.* Online: www.frontierset.org.

Galle, Jeffery and Denise P. Domizi, eds. *Faculty Learning Communities: Chancellor's Learning Scholars for Student Success*. (Lanham, MD: Rowman & Littlefield, 2021).

Gaston, Paul L. and Jerry G. Gaff. *A Guide for Curricular Change: Revising General Education*. (Washington, DC: Association of American Colleges and Universities, 2009).

Graff, Gerald and Cathy Birkenstein. *They Say / I Say: The Moves That Matter in Academic Writing*. (New York: Norton, 2014).

Granovetter, Mark S. "The Strength of Weak Ties." *American Journal of Sociology* 78, no. 6 (1973): 1360–1380. http://www.jstor.org/stable/2776392.

Gurung, Regan, Nancy Chick, and Aeron Haynie, eds. *Exploring Signature Pedagogies: Approaches to Teaching Disciplinary Habits of Mind*. (Sterling, VA: Stylus, 2009).

Hunter, M. S. "Fostering Student Learning and Success through First Year Programs." *Peer Review* 8, no. 3 (2006): 4-7.

Kuh, George. *High-Impact Educational Practices: What They Are, Who Has Access to Them, and Why They Matter*. (AAC&U, 2008).

Kuh, George, O'Donnell, K., & Reed, S. *Ensuring Quality and Taking High-Impact Practices to Scale*. (Washington DC: Association of American Colleges and Universities, 2013).

Lang, James M. *Small Teaching: Everyday Lessons from the Science of Learning*. (San Francisco: Jossey-Bass, 2016).

Lee, V. S., ed. *Teaching and Learning Through Inquiry*. (Sterling, VA: Stylus Publishing, 2004).

Linder, Kathryn E. and Chrysanthemum Mattison Hayes. *High-Impact Practices in Online Education*. (Sterling, VA: Stylus, 2018).

Liu, Eric and Nick Hanauer. *The Gardens of Democracy*. (Seattle: Sasquatch Books, 2011).

Murphy, Mary, Stephanie Fryberg, Laura Brady, Elizabeth Canning, and Cameron Hecht. Global Mindset Initiative Paper 1: Growth Mindset Cultures and Teacher Practices (August 25, 2021). Available at SSRN: https://ssrn.com/abstract=3911594.

Riordan, Tim, and James Roth, eds. *Disciplines as Frameworks for Student Learning*. (Sterling, VA: Stylus Publishing, 2005).

Routon, Wes, et al. "Dual Enrollment Pays." *Inside Higher Education*, May 2, 2022. https: //www.insidehighered.com /quicktakes /2022 /05 /02 / dual-enrollment-pays-academic-minute.

Tagg, John. *The Learning Paradigm College*. (San Francisco: Anker Publishing, 2003).

Winkelmes, M., Allison Boye, and Suzanne Tapp, eds. *Transparent Design in Higher Education*. (Sterling, VA: Stylus Publishing, 2019).

Index

Page references for figures are italicized.

About the Editors and Contributors

Lindsay Bailey is the Director of Student Affairs Strategic Technology Initiatives at the University of North Georgia. She earned her Ph.D. in college student affairs administration at the University of Georgia and has a master's in counseling. Before serving in her current position, Lindsay was the Director of Student Involvement on UNG's Oconee campus where she oversaw programming and services for student organizations and activities, leadership, diversity, and community service.

Jesse Bishop serves as the Dean of Institutional Effectiveness and Strategic Initiatives and as professor of English at Georgia Highlands College. His work focuses on using data to help shape policy, practice, and pedagogy. He holds an Ed.D. from the University of West Georgia (2015), and he is an alumnus of the Governor's Teaching Fellows (2010–2011) and the USG Executive Leadership Institute (2018–2019).

Robert R. Bleil is professor of English and Chair of the Department of Arts and Humanities at the College of Coastal Georgia. At Coastal Georgia, Rob teaches courses in composition, technical writing, American literature, American Studies, and interdisciplinary research methods. He holds a Ph.D. in English from Penn State and an M.L.S. in academic librarianship from the University of Pittsburgh.

Marlene Call is associate professor of nursing and Norcross Assessment Coordinator for Brenau University. She received her MPH in epidemiology from the University of Georgia and her Ph.D. in nursing from Augusta University. She teaches graduate and undergraduate prelicensure nursing students in community and public health nursing and is responsible for courses and workshops surrounding student success in the prelicensure nursing programs.

Jordan Cofer is the Associate Provost for Transformative Learning Experiences at Georgia College and a professor of English. He is the author of *The Gospel According to Flannery O'Connor* as well as editor of *Reconsidering Flannery O'Connor* and *Writing the Nation.* He also serves as an instructor for the AAC&U HIPs Institute.

Aubrey L. Dyer is associate professor of chemistry at Clayton State University. She received her Ph.D. in analytical chemistry from the University of Florida. Her research interests include environmental chemistry and water quality. She was a part of the second cohort of the Chancellor's Learning Scholars and is the department coordinator for the Learning Assistant program at Clayton State.

Belinda P. Edwards is professor of mathematics education in the department of secondary and middle grades mathematics (SMGE) at Kennesaw State University. Prior to teaching in the SMGE department, she taught mathematics and also coordinated the secondary mathematics teacher education program in the mathematics department. She currently teaches courses in mathematics methods and mathematics for teachers. Her research interests focus on developing equitable teaching practices to create inclusive online, hybrid, and face-to-face learning environments in higher education.

Jim Fatzinger is a visiting associate professor of management at Elon University and also teaches in the Vanderbilt School of Engineering. He has an Ed.D. from Vanderbilt's Peabody College of Education, a DBA from the University of Florida, and a MBA from the University of Miami. A 2011/2012 American Council on Education (ACE) Fellow and President of the Kentucky Chapter of the Fulbright Association, his national presentations include AACSB, AAC&U, Emory University, IUPUI, and SACSCOC. A graduate of the Harvard Institute for Management and Leadership in Education and former Presidential Fellow at Auburn University, he has published such works as his contribution to an eText entitled "A President's Perspective: The Administration of Higher Education" and a Wiley book chapter on student engagement.

Devon Fisher is Associate Dean for Teaching Innovation and Director of the Center for Teaching & Learning at Lenoir-Rhyne University. His academic interests include Victorian literature and religion. More recently, however, he has turned his attention towards developing pedagogies that support first-year students in the post-COVID-19 era.

Carl J. Gabrini is assistant professor of accounting at Dalton State College, Wright School of Business. Since joining the faculty at Dalton State, Carl's research interests have focused increasingly on topics within the Scholarship of Teaching and Learning and applied projects aimed at assisting local government and not-for-profit organizations with administrative efficiency and effectiveness issues. Carl's Ph.D. is from Florida State University, and he holds a doctoral bridge certification in accounting from the University of Florida.

Jeffery Galle served most recently as Associate Vice Chancellor for Academic Affairs in the University System of Georgia. In leadership positions in a state comprehensive university, a private research institution, and also with a large university system, Galle has enjoyed working with faculty and staff for student learning in a number of contexts.

He is the co-editor of and contributing author to *Faculty Learning Communities: Chancellor's Learning Scholars for Student Success* (2021) and *Campus Conversations: Student Success Pedagogies in Practice* (2021); co-author of *How to Be a "HIP" Campus: Maximizing Learning in Undergraduate Education*, (Satu Rogers and Jeffrey Galle, July 2015) and the co-editor and contributing author of two volumes of essays that emerged from the IPLA—*Teaching, Pedagogy, and Learning* (Rebecca Harrison and Jeffrey Galle, May 2017) and *Revitalizing Classrooms* (Jeffrey Galle and Rebecca Harrison, October 2017). Very interested in scholarship associated with place, he is also the co-editor and contributing author of *Pedagogy and Place: From the Abstract to the Quotidian* (Deric Shannon and Jeffrey Galle, June 2017). Other chapters, reviews, and conference presentations focus on innovative pedagogy for student success.

As the Scott Professor for Teaching Excellence (1996–99, ULM), the Outstanding Professor for the College of Arts and Sciences (2005, University of Louisiana at Monroe), and a Distinguished Teaching Scholar (Emory, 2009), Galle has deeply enjoyed teaching and learning with faculty, staff, and students.

Jo K. Galle served as Senior Associate Provost for Academic Affairs at Georgia Gwinnett College for thirteen years. Most recently, in 2022, she was named professor emerita for the outstanding body of work performed in her role at Georgia Gwinnett College.

Her work has included the development of over fifteen new degree programs, the establishment of over fifteen academic honor societies, and serving on over ten SACSCOC accreditation committees. She also, while at the University of Louisiana at Monroe where she was a professor of English and the Director of Assessment and Evaluation, was recognized as the Outstanding Honors Faculty (1994, 1993); the Alpha Lamba Delta favorite professor (2001, 1996); and as Who's Who Among America's Teachers (2007, 1996, 1994).

Laura Kim Gosa is assistant professor of nursing at Albany State University.

Rosa Guedes is associate professor of biology/ecology at South Georgia State College (SGSC) where she teaches biology, ecology, conservation biology, and environmental science. Her Ph.D. is in ecology from the University of Georgia (UGA). Previously, as a visiting faculty in the College of Agriculture and Environment at UGA she developed with colleagues a Study Abroad in Brazil. She was elected to Phi, Beta, Delta for her work in International Education. At SGSC she received the NISOD Excellence Award (2016), became a current member of SGSC HIPs committee, and was voted best faculty member by students the past two years in a row.

Rebecca L. Harrison is professor of English at the University of West Georgia and teaches a broad range of courses in American and women's literature, gender studies, and innovative pedagogy. Her research interests primarily center around the women authors of the U.S. South and HIP practices. She has published on writers such as Eudora Welty, Beatrice Witte Ravenel, and Julia Alvarez, work that stands alongside her co-edited book collections on cross-disciplinary inquiry-based learning strategies. Harrison currently serves as the vice president of the Eudora Welty Society and as associate editor of the *Eudora Welty Review*.

Ava Hogan-Chapman is associate professor of teacher education, clinical experience at Georgia Gwinnett College. She is a pre-service elementary clinical supervisor and teaches courses on instructional design and delivery and on characteristics for students with special needs for elementary educators in the School of Education. Her research interests converge around the topics of pre-service educator self-efficacy through experiential learning and student engagement.

Frank Holiwski is professor of psychology at South Georgia State College. He teaches Introduction to Psychology, Human Development, and Abnormal Psychology; in addition, he teaches Diversity. He earned his Ph.D. from DePaul University in Chicago. He is a graduate of the USG's Executive Leadership Institute (2014) and a recipient of a NISOD Excellence Award (2011).

Ania Kowalik is Assistant Director at the Center for Teaching Excellence at Rice University and an adjunct lecturer in the program in writing and communication. She develops professional development programs for graduate students and faculty, teaches graduate seminars in college pedagogy and the scholarship of teaching and learning, and mentors first-year undergraduate students in their transition to college. Her current research project addresses learning-centered, equitable assessment practices.

Julie Kozee is assistant professor of English at Georgia Highlands College in northwest Georgia, where she was part of the inaugural class of the University System of Georgia's Chancellor's Learning Scholars in 2018, in which she focused her faculty learning community on growth mindset and small teaching; when her term ended in 2020, she was named a Chancellor's Learning Scholar Associate as she continued her work with growth mindset in the college classroom. In 2021, she was part of a small group of select Chancellor's Learning Scholar Associates chosen to work with researchers from the Motivate Lab to develop a tool to measure the success of growth mindset initiatives in the classroom. Her primary areas of interest include disability and inclusion, growth mindset, and motivation in the freshman composition classroom, and she is currently writing a textbook focused on mindset and motivation specifically targeting first-generation, underrepresented students in the composition classroom.

Laura R. Lynch is Assistant Vice President for Faculty Affairs and professor of mathematics at the College of Coastal Georgia. She oversees the new faculty orientation process, leads the Center for Teaching and Learning, and teaches undergraduate mathematics courses. During her tenure, she has also served as a department chair and faculty senate chair. Laura received her Ph.D. in Mathematics from the University of Nebraska-Lincoln. Her current research interests include student success, academic mindsets, mathematics pedagogy, gamification, virtual reality pedagogies, game development, and faculty development.

Frank J. Mendelson is a USG Chancellor's Learning Scholar and instructor in the College of Business Administration at Savannah State University. He is a former academic director of the First-Year Experience program at SSU. His professional background is in communications and marketing, and is former Director, MBA Admissions and Interim Director, Environmental Management and Policy (MS) at Rensselaer Polytechnic Institute. He teaches First-Year Experience/Introduction to Business, Business Communications, and Principles of Marketing.

Monica Carol Miller is assistant professor of English and the Coordinator of Graduate Technical Writing Programs at Middle Georgia State University. She is the editor of *Dear Regina: Flannery O'Connor's Letters from Iowa* (2022), the co-editor of *The Tacky South* (2022), *The Routledge Companion to Literature of the U.S. South* (2022), and author of *Being Ugly:*

Southern Women Writers and Social Rebellion (2017). She teaches classes in professional and technical communication as well as American literature.

Laura Ng is professor of English and Assistant Dean of the College of Arts & Letters at the University of North Georgia on the Oconee campus. Her degree is in contemporary American literature. Her research areas include gender studies, the scholarship of teaching and learning, and peace studies. She reviews for *TLI: Teaching, Learning, Inquiry* and the *International Journal of Teaching and Learning in Higher Education.* She co-authored with Mary Carney "Scholarly Personal Narrative in the SoTL Tent," which was published in *TLI: Teaching, Learning, Inquiry.* She and Karen Redding have a chapter entitled "Moving Pictures and Words" in *Revitalizing Classrooms: Innovations and Inquiry Pedagogies in Practice.* She is a past recipient of the University of North Georgia's Distinguished Scholar for the Scholarship of Teaching and Learning.

Jessica O'Brien is Coordinator of Instructional Technology and associate librarian at Lenoir-Rhyne University in Hickory, North Carolina.

Veena Paliwal is associate professor of mathematics at University of West Georgia. Dr. Paliwal received her Ph.D. in Mathematics Education from University of Urbana-Champaign in 2013. Her research interests include early numeracy development, learning of basic number and arithmetic skills and concepts by young children, and development of mathematical concepts among pre-service teachers.

Robert L. Potter is associate professor of biology at South Georgia State College, Douglas Campus, School of Arts and Sciences. He teaches biology for STEM majors and non-STEM majors, interdisciplinary science for early childhood education, and freshwater ecosystems in the biology Bachelor of Sciences program. He earned his Ph.D. in ecology from the University of Georgia and was a member of the third cohort of the USG Chancellor's Learning Scholars Program.

Clarence E. Riley, Jr. is associate professor of health and physical education and school counselor education at Fort Valley State University. He taught previously for eight years in the Master of Public Health program. His research interests include spiritual health, epidemiology, promoting qualitative research vs. quantitative, and using innovative teaching/learning methods. His Ph.D. is in community health education from Southern Illinois University at Carbondale, M.S. Ed. in community health education from the

University of Georgia, and B.S. Ed. in health occupations education from the University of Georgia.

Sutandra Sarkar is a principal academic professional in the Department of Mathematics & Statistics at Georgia State University. She is the Precalculus Course Coordinator and the coordinator of Mathematics Assistance Complex (MAC) tutoring lab. She teaches undergraduate mathematics and statistics courses. She specializes in engaging her students across all learning modalities—both inside and outside the classroom, in face-to-face or online format, and in synchronous and asynchronous modes. Her expertise is in the field of redesigning large enrollment courses. She led the pioneering efforts of redesigning precalculus and elementary statistics courses at Georgia State University using a Modified Emporium Model. Her research interests include student engagement using educational technology and learning initiatives through global partnerships.

Stefanie Sevcik is Faculty Director for Mentored Undergraduate Research and Creative Endeavors and a lecturer in the Department of English at Georgia College & State University (GCSU). She has previously served as Faculty Champion for Community-based Engaged Learning at GCSU and as a Chancellor's Learning Scholar for the University System of Georgia. She received her Ph.D. in comparative literature from Brown University and her work on decolonization has appeared in *Research in African Literatures* and *Journal of the African Literature Association.* She has turned this critical lens to her work advocating for more diverse, equitable, and inclusive High-Impact Practices.

Shane Toepfer earned his Ph.D. in moving image studies from Georgia State University in 2011 and is currently an assistant professor of film & digital media at the University of North Georgia. His research interests include media reception, pedagogy, cultural studies, and professional wrestling and his work has appeared in edited collections on professional wrestling and sports documentaries. He is a past recipient of the UNG Oconee campus "Academic Advisor of the Year" award and currently lives in Athens, GA with his wife and two kitties.

Donna Troka is Director of Diversity and Inclusive Pedagogy at the Center for Faculty Development and Excellence at Emory University. She heads many teaching and pedagogy programs as well as academic learning communities and Inclusive Pedagogy and DEI trainings. As adjunct faculty in the Institute of Liberal Arts, she teaches special topics courses in American studies and interdisciplinary studies. Her publications include the co-edited volume *The Drag King Anthology*, and articles titled "Archivists and Faculty Collaborative Course Development" in *Provenance*, "Critical Moments: A Dialogue Toward Survival and Transformation" in *The Caribbean Review of Gender Studies*, and "'You Heard My Gun Cock': Female Agency and Aggression in Contemporary Rap Music" from *African American Research Perspectives*. Donna has a Ph.D. in interdisciplinary studies from Emory University (2007), a master's in women's studies from The Ohio State University (1998), and a BA in English from University of Illinois Urbana/Champaign (1995).

Emily G. Weigel is a Senior Academic Professional (Teaching Faculty) in the School of Biological Sciences at the Georgia Institute of Technology. She teaches at all levels of the biology curriculum, spanning lecture, laboratory, and fieldwork-based courses, as well as TA preparation training. Dr. Weigel also engages in biology education research, for which her courses and students provide data and inspiration.

Laura McCloskey Wolfe is an assistant professor/instructor of art history at the University of West Georgia. Before coming to Georgia, Laura was the recipient of an Irish Research Council Postgraduate Scholarship for Ph.D. study at Trinity College Dublin, Ireland, and her article "Exploring *Meditatio* and *Memoria* in Ireland through the *Book of Durrow*: Manuscript Illumination as the Intersection of Theological and Artistic Traditions" was nominated for a Four Courts Press Michael Adams Prize for best article or essay in Irish medieval studies. Laura also holds an M.Ed. in Multilingual and Multicultural Education and M.A. in Irish Studies. She has presented at numerous international conferences on early medieval Irish manuscript traditions, Asian and Irish poetry and artistic connections in the Victorian period, and strategies to promote college student success. She is on the editorial board of the journal *Eolas: The Journal of the American Society for Irish Medieval Studies*, has provided reviews and ancillary materials for Oxford University Press, and has also served as a lecturer for the Smithsonian Associates program in Washington, D.C.

Tyler T. Yu is the Dean of the School of Business and professor of economics and accounting at Georgia Gwinnett College. Prior to this, he was a faculty member in the School of Business at Mercer University. He has taught both graduate and undergraduate courses in business and economics. His current research interests include student success in general and undergraduate student progression, retention, and graduation in particular.

Miranda M. Zhang is a professor of finance and international studies, Associate Provost for Faculty, and Director of the Center for Teaching Excellence, at Georgia Gwinnett College (GGC). She has taught a variety of courses and received GGC's Outstanding Teaching Award in 2015 and the University System of Georgia Board of Regents Teaching Excellence Award in 2016. Her research interests include financial investment, international business, pedagogical teaching and learning, and student engagement.

Molly Zhou is professor of education in the School of Education at Dalton State College where she teaches education courses such as Contemporary and Current Issues in Education, Exploring Social & Cultural Perspectives in Education, and Exploring Teaching and Learning. Her research has focused on teacher education. She has presented nationally and internationally, and she has published extensively on culture and diversity, technology, assessment, and sustainability as they relate to teacher education and teaching and learning.